Getting Ready to Read with Readers Theatre

Getting Ready to Read with Readers Theatre

 Suzanne I. Barchers
and Charla R. Pfeffinger

Teacher Ideas Press
An imprint of Libraries Unlimited
Westport, Connecticut • London

Library of Congress Cataloging-in-Publication Data

Barchers, Suzanne I.
  Getting ready to read with readers theatre / Suzanne I. Barchers and Charla R. Pfeffinger.
    p. cm.
  Includes bibliographical references and index.
  ISBN-13: 978-1-59158-501-5 (alk. paper)
  ISBN-10: 1-59158-501-5 (alk. paper)
  1. Oral reading. 2. Reading (Elementary) 3. Readers' theater. I. Pfeffinger, Charla R. II. Title.
  LB1573.5.B37 2007
  372.45'2—dc22   2006037600

British Library Cataloguing in Publication Data is available.

Library of Congress Catalog Card Number: 2006037600
ISBN: 978-1-59158-501-5

First published in 2007

Libraries Unlimited/Teacher Ideas Press, 88 Post Road West, Westport, CT 06881
A Member of the Greenwood Publishing Group, Inc.
www.teacherideaspress.com
www.lu.com

Printed in the United States of America

The paper used in this book complies with the
Permanent Paper Standard issued by the National
Information Standards Organization (Z39.48–1984).

10 9 8 7 6 5 4 3 2 1

Contents

Introduction

The Role of Readers Theatre

"Readers theatre is a presentation by two or more participants who read from scripts and interpret a literary work in such a way that the audience imaginatively senses characterization, setting, and action. Voice and body tension rather than movement are involved, thus eliminating the need for the many practice sessions that timing and action techniques require in the presentation of a play" (Laughlin and Latrobe 1990, 3). Traditionally, the primary focus in readers theatre is on an effective reading of the script rather than on a dramatic, memorized presentation. Generally, there are minimal props and movement on the stage, although with young students, adding such touches enlivens the production and invites more active participation. The ease of incorporating readers theatre in the reading program offers teachers an exciting way to build fluency and automaticity into reading instruction.

The scripts in this collection were developed from nursery rhymes, clapping rhymes, jumping rhymes, and songs. Most scripts have a readability ranges from 0.0 to .5 according to an evaluation using the Flesh-Kincaid readability scale. A few are more difficult and are noted; none exceeds a score of .9. They scripts are grouped thematically, consistent with themes found in kindergarten and first grade. Although all are easy, each script should be further evaluated by the teacher for features that will assist easy reading: familiarity, rhyme, rhythm, repetition, predictability, and so forth. Though children are not expected to memorize the lines in readers theatre, many children will internalize the lines because of their familiarity with many of the rhymes and will need only the slightest prompting from the script after adequate practice time. Such success in reading and sharing is highly motivating for the beginning reader. An additional benefit is the pleasure of performing for adults or other classes and the ease of using a script for special days when a program is expected.

Several of the scripts give opportunities for the audience to chime in with lines. This promotes active listening among the audience members. Specific notes for the scripts suggest those scripts that lend themselves to this practice. In addition, cue cards could be used to prompt the audience. Alternatively, the audience can be instructed as to the lines and be told to watch a particular student for the cue to say the lines.

Preparing the Scripts

Once scripts are chosen for reading, make enough copies for each reader, plus an extra set or two for your use and a replacement copy. To help readers keep their place, use color highlighters when preparing the scripts. For example, someone reading the role of Reader 1 could have the words "Reader 1" highlighted in blue, with "Reader 2" highlighted in yellow on another copy. This helps readers track their parts and eases management of the scripts.

Photocopied scripts will last longer if you use a three-hole punch (or copy them on pre-punched paper) and place them in inexpensive folders. The folders can be color-coordinated to the internal highlighting for each reader's part. The title of the play can be printed on the outside of the folder, and scripts can be stored easily for the next reading. The preparation of the scripts is a good project for a student aide or volunteer parent. The preparation takes a minimum of initial attention and needs to be repeated only when a folder is lost.

You may want to customize your scripts. For example, it may be more convenient to have four readers instead of eight. Photocopy the script and use removable peel-and-press labels to designate different readers. If you add verses to the script, ask a volunteer to retype the entire script, incorporating the new verses.

Getting Started

For the first experience with a readers theatre script, choose a script with many readers to involve more students. Gather the students informally, perhaps in a circle on the floor. Read aloud the traditional version of either the nursery rhyme, the song, or the script itself. If a picture book version is available, such as for "Old Mother Hubbard," read the book aloud. Next, introduce the script and explain that readers theatre does not mean memorizing a play and acting it out, but rather reading a script aloud with perhaps a few props and actions. Read aloud the entire script, allowing students to join in spontaneously. Many of the scripts are predictable, and students will naturally chime in. (See the introduction to each chapter for additional recommendations for each script.)

Select volunteers to do the initial reading, allowing them an opportunity to review their parts before reading aloud. Discuss how the scripts are alike or different from nursery rhymes or songs that the students have heard. Write harder words on the board and review their meaning as necessary. While these students are preparing to read their script, another group could be reviewing another script or brainstorming ideas for props or staging, if desired.

Once the students have read the scripts and become familiar with the new vocabulary, determine which students will read the various parts for a more formal performance. Some parts are considerably more demanding than others, and students should be encouraged to volunteer for roles that will be comfortable. Once they are familiar with readers theatre, students should be encouraged to stretch and try a reading that is challenging.

Once a few scripts are prepared, think about how to expand the experience. A readers theatre workshop could be held periodically, with each student belonging to a group that prepares a script for presentation. A readers theatre festival could be planned for a special day when several short scripts are presented consecutively, with brief intermissions between each reading. Consider grouping together related scripts from the chapter themes. They could be broken down further, such as having all counting scripts, all insect scripts, all song-based scripts, and the like. If you present scripts to adults, consider placing in a program the historical notes provided in the chapter introductions for many of the scripts. See references at the end of this section for recommending reading on the history of nursery rhymes.

Presentation Suggestions

For readers theatre, readers traditionally stand—or sit on stools, chairs, or the floor—in a formal presentation style. The narrators may stand with the script placed on music stands or lecterns slightly off to one or both sides. The readers may hold their scripts in black or colored folders. Because these scripts are intended for the very youngest readers—and are short—the presentation can be less formal. It is likely that the students will quickly memorize their lines and use the script only incidentally.

Props

Readers theatre has no, or few, props. However, simple costuming effects, such as wearing certain colors, plus a few props on stage will lend interest to the presentation. A few suggestions for simple props or costuming are included; however, the students should be encouraged to decide how much or how little to add to their reading. Examining collections of nursery rhymes may give students ideas for enhancements. However, the use of props or actions may be distracting for beginning readers, and the emphasis should remain on the reading rather than on an overly complicated presentation.

Delivery Suggestions

Delivery suggestions are not imbedded in the scripts. Therefore, it is important to discuss with the students what will make the scripts come alive as they read. A variety of warm-ups can help students with expression. For example, have the entire class respond to the following:

- Finding a present on your bed

- Being grounded for something a sibling did

- Learning that a best friend is moving

- Getting a new puppy or kitten

- Discovering a sibling ate your last piece of birthday cake

- Having a genie or fairy appear with three wishes

Simple actions can also be incorporated into readers theatre. Encourage presenters to use action in addition to expression by practicing pantomime in groups. Introduce mime by having students try the following familiar actions: combing hair, brushing teeth, turning the pages of a book, eating an ice cream cone, making a phone call, falling asleep. Then select and try various activities drawn from the scripts.

Some of the scripts are based on familiar tunes, such as "The Bear Went over the Mountain," which is the same as "For He's a Jolly Good Fellow." The use of music can enhance the delivery of the play. Introduce lively scripts with lively music. Add rhythm instruments where appropriate.

During their first experiences with presenting a script, students are tempted to keep their heads buried in the script, making sure they don't miss a line. Students should learn the material well enough to look up from the script during the presentation. Students can learn to use onstage focus—to look at each other during the presentation. This is most logical for readers who are interacting with each other. The use of offstage focus—the presenters look directly into the eyes of the audience—is more logical for the readers who are uninvolved with other readers. Alternatively, have students who do not interact with each other focus on a prearranged offstage location, such as the classroom clock, during delivery. Generally, the audience should be able to see the readers' facial expressions during the reading.

The Audience

When students are part of the audience, they should understand their role. Rehearse good listening practices, plus applauding. Ask students to think about how they would want the audience to react to the reading. Brainstorm what might go wrong during a reading and how to react positively or patiently in these situations.

The Next Step

Once students have enjoyed the reading process involved in preparing and presenting readers theatre, the logical next step is to involve them in the writing process by creating their own scripts. Recommendations for additional verses are included in the chapter introductions.

Readers Theatre Online Resources

www.storycart.com

www.aaronshep.com/rt/

http://scriptsforschools.com/

References and Resources

Barchers, Suzanne I. *Readers Theatre for Beginning Readers*. Westport, CT: Teacher Ideas Press, 1993.

Laughlin, Mildred Knight, and Kathy Howard Latrobe. *Readers Theatre for Children: Scripts and Script Development*. Westport, CT: Teacher Ideas Press, 1990.

Opie, Iona, and Peter Opie, eds. *The Oxford Dictionary of Nursery Rhymes*. New York: Oxford University Press, 1997.

Roberts, Chris. *Heavy Words Lightly Thrown: The Reason Behind the Rhyme*. New York: Gotham Books, 2005.

Adapted from Readers Theatre for Beginning Readers *by Suzanne I. Barchers. Westport, CT: Teacher Ideas Press, 1993.*

Chapter One

The Alphabet, Counting, Colors, and Time

There are many opportunities to incorporate these scripts into your curriculum, especially when learning the alphabet, counting, and so forth. Students may be familiar with a few of the rhymes that serve as the basis for the scripts, such as "One, Two, Buckle My Shoe" or "Three Blind Mice." These would serve as a good starting point for this section of scripts. The following suggestions are organized thematically.

Alphabet Scripts

A Was an Archer

Liberally adapted from a rhyme that appeared in a book for children in England in the early 1700s, this script offers opportunities for students to suggest other words for each of the alphabet letters, in themes such as food or animals.

A is for apple that turned bright red.
B is for butter that I put on my bread.
A is for anteater that loves to eat ants.
B is for butterfly that loves to visit plants.

Consider having each reader wear a placard that lists his or her related letter of the alphabet. *Historical note:* Variations of this rhyme appeared in America, in Boston, as early as 1750. Illustrated versions appeared in the 1800s, with variants remaining a popular rhyme throughout the century.

Great A, Little a

Use this adaptation of the rhyme from the 1800s to reinforce uppercase and lowercase letters. Brainstorm other people, animals, or insects that could be in the cupboard. The script of twenty-six lines has been divided so that thirteen readers have two lines each. If preferred, the script could have twenty-six readers, with each reading one line. If available, place a cupboard by the readers and have students pantomime the actions. *Historical note:* Early printers of books for children included this rhyme, with John Newbery including a version in *A Little Pretty Pocket-Book* (1744).

Her Name Is Allie

Create new rhymes using your students' names. If there is no rhyming word for a name, consider using a nonsense word. One caution: if creating a new rhyme for a name might lead to teasing, use the original script. Alternatively, consider creating a new set of verses using animal names, with just lines two and three rhyming to make it easier to develop.

His name is Al, Al, Al.
He's an alligator, 'gator 'gator.
See you later, later, later.
His name is Al.

Counting Scripts

1, 2, 3, 4, 5

This script, which could also be used with scripts about animals, provides the opportunity to practice counting from one to fifty and back again. Have the students practice their lines, emphasizing the final syllable on numbers such as twenty to facilitate the rhymes (*twenty* and *tree*). As with other long scripts, reconfigure the number of readers, as preferred. To enliven the presentation, have another student sit on the floor in front of each reader. As the reader states a number, have a student hold up a corresponding number card. *Historical note:* The first four lines were recorded in 1765, with a variations published through the next two hundred years.

The Ants Go Marching

Most of the lines of this script repeat from verse to verse. The last line—BOOM! BOOM! BOOM!—provides an opportunity for audience participation. Explain and rehearse this line with the audience. Have Reader Six gesture to the audience to say the line, or fulfill this role as leader yourself. If performing the script for youngsters, consider having them pound their hands on their laps or their feet on the floor while saying the line. If you wish to have a longer performance, work backward through the script, starting with nine after the last verse is read. The lines can be sung to "When Johnny Comes Marching Home Again."

I Saw Three Ships

Some students may connect this with a Christmas song. This version builds on a New Year's theme, with variations that increase to ten ships and ten sailors. For an interesting math problem, compute how many ships there were in total (fifty-two). Students could write verses for one and two ships as well. Provide sailor hats for the students to wear. *Historical note:* An earlier version appears in John Forbes's *Cantus: Songs and Fancies,* published in Aberdeen, Scotland, in 1666.

One, Two, Buckle My Shoe

This variation on a familiar counting rhyme provides abundant practice with counting from one to ten. Have reader ten read "Can't do it again" sleepily, indicating to the audience that the script has concluded. Shoes can be placed on stage for props. *Historical note:* One version appears in Massachusetts as early as 1780, with another version continuing to thirty.

Ten Green Frogs

Except for a slight variation at the end, the first line is the only one that changes in this script, starting with ten green frogs and ending with none. To add visual interest to this script, have ten nonspeaking parts—ten students who sit cross-legged on the floor, exiting as indicated by each verse. If preferred, have the audience participate by joining readers five and six in saying "Yum, yum…." Students can be dressed in green.

Three Blind Mice

The variations on this familiar round capitalize on alliteration and rhyme for the variations with the additional verses. Students could write verses for one and two mice. *Historical note:* Thomas Ravenscroft, a chorister at St. Paul's Cathedral in London, included an early version of this round in a collection in 1609, *The Seconde part of Musicks melodie.*

Colors

Chalk on the Walk

For this script, consider having six nonspeaking roles, students who sit on the floor and hold up the corresponding colors when Readers Five and Six recount the colors (red, pink, yellow, blue, green, and purple). Caution Readers Five and Six to say the colors slowly to allow time for the colors to be held aloft. For a variation, have the students choose a new group of colors. Consider having the audience practice saying the list of colors, recounting them with along with Readers Five and Six. The colors could be listed on a poster board in the same order for reference.

Time

Good Morning

Use this script to help students as they become more familiar with the times of the day. The repetitive lines provide an opportunity for audience participation. For simple decorations, use a clock theme. Draw clocks on poster board to go with the appropriate times of the day.

A Was an Archer

Reader One: A was an archer
Reader Two: Who shot at a frog.
Reader Three: B was a butcher
Reader Four: Who had a great dog.

Reader Five: C was a captain
Reader Six: Who went out to sea.
Reader Seven: D was my daddy
Reader Eight: Who liked to drink tea.

Reader One: E was an elf
Reader Two: Who lived under a flower.
Reader Three: F was a farmer
Reader Four: Who had a great tower.

Reader Five: G was a gal
Reader Six: Who had bad luck.
Reader Seven: H was a hunter
Reader Eight: Who hunted a buck.

Reader One: I was an Indian
Reader Two: Who was very tall.
Reader Three: J was a juggler
Reader Four: Who tossed up balls.

Reader Five: K was a king
Reader Six: Who ruled the land.
Reader Seven: L was his lady
Reader Eight: Who gave him a hand.

Reader One: M was a maid
Reader Two: Who cleaned up the house.
Reader Three: N was a nanny
Reader Four: Who screamed at a mouse.

Reader Five: O was an orator
Reader Six: Who really liked to talk.
Reader Seven: P was a preacher
Reader Eight: Who could talk and could walk.

Reader One: Q was a queen
Reader Two: Who lived all alone.
Reader Three: R was a repairman
Reader Four: Who fixed our broken phone.

Reader Five: S was a singer
Reader Six: Who loved to sing.
Reader Seven: T was a teacher
Reader Eight: Who had lots of zing.

Reader One: U was an uncle
Reader Two: Who could only sigh.
Reader Three: V was a vixen
Reader Four: Who was very sly.

Reader Five: W was a waitress
Reader Six: Who carried a tray.
Reader Seven: X he took x-rays
Reader Eight: and did it his way.

Reader One: Y was a youth
Reader Two: Who never grew old.
Reader Three: Z was a zany person
Reader Four: Who loved to be bold.

Great A, Little a

Reader One: Great A, little a, bouncing B!
The cat's in the cupboard, and she can't see.

Reader Two: Great C, little c, bouncing D!
The dog's in the cupboard, and he has the key.

Reader Three: Great E, little e, bouncing F!
A man's in the cupboard, and he is a chef.

Reader Four: Great G, little g, bouncing H!
A boy's in the cupboard, and he wants a plate.

Reader Five: Great I, little I, bouncing J!
A mouse is in the cupboard, and it is gray.

Reader Six: Great K, little k, bouncing L!
A cook's in the cupboard, with good food to smell.

Reader Seven: Great M, little m, bouncing N!
A chick's in the cupboard, looking for a hen.

Reader Eight: Great O, little o, bouncing P!
A mom's in the cupboard, looking for tea.

Reader Nine: Great Q, little q, bouncing R!
A girl's in the cupboard, looking for a jar.

Reader Ten: Great S, little s, bouncing T!
A grandma's in the cupboard, looking for peas.

Reader Eleven: Great U, little u, bouncing V!

An ant's in the cupboard, wanting food that's free.

Reader Twelve: Great W, little w, bouncing X!

A grandpa's in the cupboard. He's lost his specks.

Reader Thirteen: Great Y, little y, bouncing Z!

Close the cupboard. One, two, three.

 # Her Name Is Allie

Reader One: Her name is Allie, Allie, Allie.
Reader Two: Her aunt is Sally, Sally, Sally.
Reader Three: She lives in a valley, valley, valley.
Reader Four: Her name is Allie.

Reader One: His name is Ben, Ben, Ben.
Reader Two: He has a hen, hen, hen.
Reader Three: It lives in a pen, pen, pen.
Reader Four: His name is Ben.

Reader One: Her name is Candy, Candy, Candy.
Reader Two: Her dad is Andy, Andy, Andy.
Reader Three: She is so handy, handy, handy.
Reader Four: Her name is Candy.

Reader One: His name is Dawson, Dawson, Dawson.
Reader Two: He hit a home run, home run, home run.
Reader Three: It was awesome, awesome, awesome.
Reader Four: His name is Dawson.

Reader One: His name is Eddie, Eddie, Eddie.
Reader Two: His dad is Freddie, Freddie, Freddie.
Reader Three: He has a new teddy, teddy, teddy.
Reader Four: His name is Eddie.

Reader One: His name is Frank, Frank, Frank.
Reader Two: His dad runs a bank, bank, bank.
Reader Three: He can drive a tank, tank, tank.
Reader Four: His name is Frank.

Reader One: His name is Greg, Greg, Greg.
Reader Two: His mother is Peg, Peg, Peg.
Reader Three: He broke his leg, leg, leg.
Reader Four: His name is Greg.

Reader One: His name is Hunter, Hunter, Hunter
Reader Two: He is a punter, punter, punter.
Reader Three: He can't be blunter, blunter, blunter.
Reader Four: His name is Hunter.

Reader One: His name is Ike, Ike, Ike.
Reader Two: He likes to hike, hike, hike.
Reader Three: He rides his bike, bike, bike.
Reader Four: His name is Ike.

Reader One: Her name is Jane, Jane, Jane.
Reader Two: She loves the rain, rain, rain.
Reader Three: She is not plain, plain, plain.
Reader Four: Her name is Jane.

Reader One: His name is Kent, Kent, Kent.
Reader Two: He has a dent, dent, dent.
Reader Three: In his tent, tent, tent.
Reader Four: His name is Kent.

Reader One: His name is Larry, Larry, Larry.
Reader Two: His brother is Jerry, Jerry, Jerry.
Reader Three: He is very merry, merry, merry.
Reader Four: His name is Larry.

Reader One: Her name is Mary. Mary, Mary.
Reader Two: Her dad is Barry, Barry, Barry.
Reader Three: He runs a dairy, dairy, dairy.
Reader Four: Her name is Mary.

Reader One: His name is Ned, Ned, Ned.
Reader Two: He likes to wear red, red, red.
Reader Three: He loves to eat bread, bread, bread.
Reader Four: His name is Ned.

Reader One: His name is Owen, Owen, Owen.
Reader Two: He's really glowing, glowing, glowing.
Reader Three: Because he's growing, growing, growing.
Reader Four: His name is Owen.

Reader One: Her name is Pat, Pat, Pat.
Reader Two: She has a cat, cat, cat.
Reader Three: She wears a blue hat, hat, hat.
Reader Four: Her name is Pat.

Reader One: His name is Quinn, Quinn, Quinn.
Reader Two: His sister is Lynn, Lynn, Lynn.
Reader Three: He loves to spin, spin, spin.
Reader Four: His name is Quinn.

Reader One: Her name is Rori, Rori, Rori.
Reader Two: Her mother is Cory, Cory, Cory.
Reader Three: She can tell a story, story, story.
Reader Four: Her name is Rori.

Reader One: His name is Steve, Steve, Steve.
Reader Two: What's up his sleeve, sleeve, sleeve?
Reader Three: He is going to leave, leave, leave.
Reader Four: His name is Steve.

Reader One: His name is Tad, Tad, Tad.
Reader Two: He is a good lad, lad, lad.
Reader Three: He can never be bad, bad, bad.
Reader Four: His name is Tad.

Reader One: Her name is Uma, Uma, Uma.
Reader Two: She lives in Yuma, Yuma, Yuma.
Reader Three: She rides a puma, puma, puma.
Reader Four: Her name is Uma.

Reader One: His name is Vern, Vern, Vern,
Reader Two: His sister is Fern, Fern, Fern.
Reader Three: He loves to learn, learn, learn.
Reader Four: His name is Vern.

Reader One: His name is Wes, Wes, Wes.
Reader Two: He loves to play chess, chess, chess.
Reader Three: His room is a mess, mess, mess.
Reader Four: His name is Wes.

Reader One: His name is Xavier, Xavier, Xavier.
Reader Two: Lemon is his flavor, flavor, flavor.
Reader Three: He hates to labor, labor, labor.
Reader Four: His name is Xavier.

Reader One: Her name is Yvette, Yvette, Yvette.
Reader Two: Her dad is Brett, Brett, Brett.
Reader Three: He flies a jet, jet, jet.
Reader Four: Her name is Yvette.

Reader One: His name is Zack, Zack, Zack.
Reader Two: His dad is Jack, Jack, Jack.
Reader Three: His brother is Mack, Mack, Mack.
Reader Four: His name is Zack.

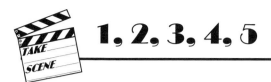

Reader One: 1, 2, 3, 4, 5.
Reader Two: I caught a hare alive.
Reader Three: 6, 7, 8, 9, 10.
Reader Four: I let her go again.

Reader Five: 11, 12, 13, 14, 15.
Reader Six: I caught a snake that's green.
Reader Seven: 16, 17, 18, 19, 20.
Reader Eight: I let the snake go free.

Reader One: 21, 22, 23, 24, 25.
Reader Two: I caught a fish in a dive.
Reader Three: 26, 27, 28, 29, 30.
Reader Four: I let it go in the sea.

Reader Five: 31, 32, 33, 34, 35.
Reader Six: I caught a bee from a hive.
Reader Seven: 36, 37, 38, 39, 40.
Reader Eight: I let the bumblebee flee.

Reader One: 41, 42, 43, 44, 45.
Reader Two: I caught a bird that was live.
Reader Three: 46, 47, 48, 49, 50.
Reader Four: I let the bird fly to the tree.

Reader Five: 50, 49, 48, 47, 46.
Reader Six: I caught two cute chicks.
Reader Seven: 45, 44, 43, 42, 41.
Reader Eight: I let them play in the sun.

Reader One: 40, 39, 38, 37, 36.
Reader Two: I caught a dog with ticks.
Reader Three: 35, 34, 33, 32, 31.
Reader Four: I knew the dog wanted none.

Reader Five: 30, 29, 28, 27, 26.
Reader Six: I caught a cat that did tricks.
Reader Seven: 25, 24, 23, 22, 21.
Reader Eight: I let the cat have lots of fun.

Reader One: 20, 19, 18, 17, 16,
Reader Two: I caught the biggest fox I've seen.
Reader Three: 15, 14, 13, 12, 11.
Reader Four: I let the fox go to its den.

Reader Five: 10, 9, 8, 7, 6.
Reader Six: Now you have heard all my tricks.
Reader Seven: 5, 4, 3, 2, 1.
Reader Eight: And now my counting's all done.

The Ants Go Marching

Reader One: The ants go marching one by one, hurrah, hurrah.

Reader Two: The ants go marching one by one, hurrah, hurrah.

Reader Three: The ants go marching one by one.

Reader Four: The little one stops to suck his thumb.

Reader Five: And they all go marching down to the ground.

Reader Six: To get out of the rain.

Audience: BOOM! BOOM! BOOM!

Reader One: The ants go marching two by two, hurrah, hurrah.

Reader Two: The ants go marching two by two, hurrah, hurrah.

Reader Three: The ants go marching two by two.

Reader Four: The little one stops to tie his shoe.

Reader Five: And they all go marching down to the ground.

Reader Six: To get out of the rain.

Audience: BOOM! BOOM! BOOM!

Reader One: The ants go marching three by three, hurrah, hurrah.

Reader Two: The ants go marching three by three, hurrah, hurrah.

Reader Three: The ants go marching three by three.

Reader Four: The little one stops to climb a tree.

Reader Five: And they all go marching down to the ground.

Reader Six: To get out of the rain.

Audience: BOOM! BOOM! BOOM!

Reader One: The ants go marching four by four, hurrah, hurrah.

Reader Two: The ants go marching four by four, hurrah, hurrah.

Reader Three: The ants go marching four by four.

Reader Four: The little one stops to shut the door.

Reader Five: And they all go marching down to the ground.

Reader Six: To get out of the rain.

Audience: BOOM! BOOM! BOOM!

Reader One: The ants go marching five by five, hurrah, hurrah.
Reader Two: The ants go marching five by five, hurrah, hurrah.
Reader Three: The ants go marching five by five.
Reader Four: The little one stops to take a drive.
Reader Five: And they all go marching down to the ground.
Reader Six: To get out of the rain.
Audience: BOOM! BOOM! BOOM!

Reader One: The ants go marching six by six, hurrah, hurrah.
Reader Two: The ants go marching six by six, hurrah, hurrah.
Reader Three: The ants go marching six by six.
Reader Four: The little one stops to pick up sticks.
Reader Five: And they all go marching down to the ground.
Reader Six: To get out of the rain.
Audience: BOOM! BOOM! BOOM!

Reader One: The ants go marching seven by seven, hurrah, hurrah.
Reader Two: The ants go marching seven by seven, hurrah, hurrah.
Reader Three: The ants go marching seven by seven.
Reader Four: The little one stops to pray to heaven.
Reader Five: And they all go marching down to the ground.
Reader Six: To get out of the rain.
Audience: BOOM! BOOM! BOOM!

Reader One: The ants go marching eight by eight, hurrah, hurrah.
Reader Two: The ants go marching eight by eight, hurrah, hurrah.
Reader Three: The ants go marching eight by eight.
Reader Four: The little one stops to shut the gate.
Reader Five: And they all go marching down to the ground.
Reader Six: To get out of the rain.
Audience: BOOM! BOOM! BOOM!

Reader One: The ants go marching nine by nine, hurrah, hurrah.

Reader Two: The ants go marching nine by nine, hurrah, hurrah.

Reader Three: The ants go marching nine by nine.

Reader Four: The little one stops to check the time.

Reader Five: And they all go marching down to the ground.

Reader Six: To get out of the rain.

Audience: BOOM! BOOM! BOOM!

Reader One: The ants go marching ten by ten, hurrah, hurrah.

Reader Two: The ants go marching ten by ten, hurrah, hurrah.

Reader Three: The ants go marching ten by ten.

Reader Four: The little one stops to say "THE END."

Reader Five: And they all go marching down to the ground.

Reader Six: To get out of the rain.

Audience: BOOM! BOOM! BOOM!

I Saw Three Ships

Reader One: I saw three ships come sailing in.

Reader Two: On New Year's Day, on New Year's Day.

Reader Three: I saw three ships come sailing in.

Reader Four: On New Year's Day in the morning.

Reader Five: What do you think was in them then?

Reader Six: Was in them then, was in them then?

Reader Seven: And what do you think was in them then?

Reader Eight: On New Year's Day in the morning.

Reader One: Three pretty girls were in them then,

Reader Two: Were in them then, were in them then.

Reader Three: Three pretty girls were in them then,

Reader Four: On New Year's Day in the morning.

Reader Five: One girl could whistle. One girl could sing.

Reader Six: One girl could play the violin.

Reader Seven: Such joy there was on New Year's Day,

Reader Eight: On New Year's Day in the morning.

Reader One: I saw four ships come sailing in.

Reader Two: On New Year's Day, on New Year's Day.

Reader Three: I saw four ships come sailing in.

Reader Four: On New Year's Day in the morning.

Reader Five: What do you think was in them then?

Reader Six: Was in them then, was in them then?

Reader Seven: And what do you think was in them then?

Reader Eight: On New Year's Day in the morning.

Reader One: Four tall men were in them then,
Reader Two: Were in them then, were in them then.
Reader Three: Four tall men were in them then,
Reader Four: On New Year's Day in the morning.
Reader Five: One man could bake. One man could write.
Reader Six: Two men loved to fly a kite.
Reader Seven: Such joy there was on New Year's Day,
Reader Eight: On New Year's Day in the morning.

Reader One: I saw five ships come sailing in.
Reader Two: On New Year's Day, on New Year's Day.
Reader Three: I saw five ships come sailing in.
Reader Four: On New Year's Day in the morning.
Reader Five: What do you think was in them then?
Reader Six: Was in them then, was in them then?
Reader Seven: And what do you think was in them then?
Reader Eight: On New Year's Day in the morning.

Reader One: Five big dogs were in them then,
Reader Two: Were in them then, were in them then.
Reader Three: Five big dogs were in them then,
Reader Four: On New Year's Day in the morning.
Reader Five: One dog could bark. Two dogs could jump.
Reader Six: Three dog's tails went thump, thump, thump.
Reader Seven: Such joy there was on New Year's Day,
Reader Eight: On New Year's Day in the morning.

Reader One: I saw six ships come sailing in.
Reader Two: On New Year's Day, on New Year's Day.
Reader Three: I saw six ships come sailing in.
Reader Four: On New Year's Day in the morning.
Reader Five: What do you think was in them then?
Reader Six: Was in them then, was in them then?
Reader Seven: And what do you think was in them then?
Reader Eight: On New Year's Day in the morning.

Reader One: Six furry cats were in them then,
Reader Two: Were in them then, were in them then.
Reader Three: Six furry cats were in them then,
Reader Four: On New Year's Day in the morning.
Reader Five: One cat could mew. Two cats could purr.
Reader Six: Four cats liked to lick their fur.
Reader Seven: Such joy there was on New Year's Day,
Reader Eight: On New Year's Day in the morning.

Reader One: I saw seven ships come sailing in
Reader Two: On New Year's Day, on New Year's Day.
Reader Three: I saw seven ships come sailing in.
Reader Four: On New Year's Day in the morning.
Reader Five: What do you think was in them then?
Reader Six: Was in them then, was in them then?
Reader Seven: And what do you think was in them then?
Reader Eight: On New Year's Day in the morning.

Reader One: Seven funny clowns were in them then,
Reader Two: Were in them then, were in them then.
Reader Three: Seven funny clowns were in them then,
Reader Four: On New Year's Day in the morning.
Reader Five: One clown could smile. Two clowns could frown.
Reader Six: Four clowns wore their pants upside down.
Reader Seven: Such joy there was on New Year's Day,
Reader Eight: On New Year's Day in the morning.

Reader One: I saw eight ships come sailing in.
Reader Two: On New Year's Day, on New Year's Day.
Reader Three: I saw eight ships come sailing in.
Reader Four: On New Year's Day in the morning.
Reader Five: What do you think was in them then?
Reader Six: Was in them then, was in them then?
Reader Seven: And what do you think was in them then?
Reader Eight: On New Year's Day in the morning.

Reader One: Eight little boys were in them then,
Reader Two: Were in them then, were in them then.
Reader Three: Eight little boys were in them then,
Reader Four: On New Year's Day in the morning.
Reader Five: One boy could jump. Two boys could skip.
Reader Six: Five boys could do a back flip.
Reader Seven: Such joy there was on New Year's Day,
Reader Eight: On New Year's Day in the morning.

Reader One: I saw nine ships come sailing in.
Reader Two: On New Year's Day, on New Year's Day.
Reader Three: I saw nine ships come sailing in.
Reader Four: On New Year's Day in the morning.
Reader Five: What do you think was in them then?
Reader Six: Was in them then, was in them then?
Reader Seven: And what do you think was in them then?
Reader Eight: On New Year's Day in the morning.

Reader One: Nine fat babies were in them then,
Reader Two: Were in them then, were in them then.
Reader Three: Nine fat babies were in them then,
Reader Four: On New Year's Day in the morning.
Reader Five: One baby could scoot. Two babies could crawl.
Reader Six: Six babies could catch a big blue ball.
Reader Seven: Such joy there was on New Year's Day,
Reader Eight: On New Year's Day in the morning.

Reader One: I saw ten ships come sailing in.
Reader Two: On New Year's Day, on New Year's Day.
Reader Three: I saw ten ships come sailing in.
Reader Four: On New Year's Day in the morning.
Reader Five: What do you think was in them then?
Reader Six: Was in them then, was in them then?
Reader Seven: And what do you think was in them then?
Reader Eight: On New Year's Day in the morning.

Reader One: Ten fine sailors were in them then,

Reader Two: Were in them then, were in them then.

Reader Three: Ten fine sailors were in them then,

Reader Four: On New Year's Day in the morning.

Reader Five: One sailor could steer. Two sailors could tack.

Reader Six: Seven sailors said "Let's go back!"

Reader Seven: Such joy there was on New Year's Day,

Reader Eight: On New Year's Day in the morning.

One, Two, Buckle My Shoe

Reader One: One, two
Reader Two: Buckle my shoe.
Reader Three: Three, four
Reader Four: Shut the door.
Reader Five: Five, six
Reader Six: Pick up sticks.
Reader Seven: Seven, eight
Reader Eight: Lay them straight.
Reader Nine: Nine, ten
Reader Ten: Do it again.

Reader One: One, two
Reader Two: What will I do?
Reader Three: Three, four
Reader Four: Mop the floor.
Reader Five: Five, six
Reader Six: Fix a cake mix.
Reader Seven: Seven, eight
Reader Eight: Let it bake.
Reader Nine: Nine, ten
Reader Ten: Do it again.

Reader One: One, two
Reader Two: I love the zoo.
Reader Three: Three, four
Reader Four: Hear the lion roar?
Reader Five: Five, six
Reader Six: See the baby chicks?
Reader Seven: Seven, eight
Reader Eight: It is all so great.
Reader Nine: Nine, ten
Reader Ten: Do it again.

Reader One: One, two

Reader Two: How big I grew!

Reader Three: Three, four

Reader Four: I will grow more.

Reader Five: Five, six

Reader Six: I can do tricks.

Reader Seven: Seven, eight

Reader Eight: On my skates.

Reader Nine: Nine, ten

Reader Ten: Do it again.

Reader One: One, two

Reader Two: The sky is blue.

Reader Three: Three, four

Reader Four: Let's go to the store.

Reader Five: Five, six

Reader Six: Some ice cream I'll pick.

Reader Seven: Seven, eight

Reader Eight: I can't wait.

Reader Nine: Nine, ten

Reader Ten: Do it again.

Reader One: One, two

Reader Two: I love you.

Reader Three: Three, four

Reader Four: Do you love me more?

Reader Five: Five, six

Reader Six: Hug me quick.

Reader Seven: Seven, eight

Reader Eight: It's very late.

Reader Nine: Nine, ten

Reader Ten: Can't do it again.

Ten Green Frogs

Reader One: Ten green frogs

Reader Two: Sat on a log

Reader Three: Eating the most

Reader Four: Delicious bugs.

Reader Five: Yum, yum, yum, yum.

Reader Six: Yum, yum, yum!

Reader Seven: One jumped in the pool

Reader Eight: Where it was nice and cool.

Reader One: Nine green frogs

Reader Two: Sat on a log

Reader Three: Eating the most

Reader Four: Delicious bugs.

Reader Five: Yum, yum, yum, yum.

Reader Six: Yum, yum, yum!

Reader Seven: One jumped in the pool

Reader Eight: Where it was nice and cool.

Reader One: Eight green frogs

Reader Two: Sat on a log

Reader Three: Eating the most

Reader Four: Delicious bugs.

Reader Five: Yum, yum, yum, yum.

Reader Six: Yum, yum, yum!

Reader Seven: One jumped in the pool

Reader Eight: Where it was nice and cool.

Reader One: Seven green frogs

Reader Two: Sat on a log

Reader Three: Eating the most

Reader Four: Delicious bugs.

Reader Five: Yum, yum, yum, yum.
Reader Six: Yum, yum, yum!
Reader Seven: One jumped in the pool
Reader Eight: Where it was nice and cool.

Reader One: Six green frogs
Reader Two: Sat on a log
Reader Three: Eating the most
Reader Four: Delicious bugs.
Reader Five: Yum, yum, yum, yum.
Reader Six: Yum, yum, yum!
Reader Seven: One jumped in the pool
Reader Eight: Where it was nice and cool.

Reader One: Five green frogs
Reader Two: Sat on a log
Reader Three: Eating the most
Reader Four: Delicious bugs.
Reader Five: Yum yum!
Reader Five: Yum, yum, yum, yum.
Reader Six: Yum, yum, yum!
Reader Seven: One jumped in the pool
Reader Eight: Where it was nice and cool.

Reader One: Four green frogs
Reader Two: Sat on a log
Reader Three: Eating the most
Reader Four: Delicious bugs.
Reader Five: Yum, yum, yum, yum.
Reader Six: Yum, yum, yum!
Reader Seven: One jumped in the pool
Reader Eight: Where it was nice and cool.

Reader One: Three green frogs
Reader Two: Sat on a log
Reader Three: Eating the most
Reader Four: Delicious bugs.
Reader Five: Yum, yum, yum, yum.
Reader Six: Yum, yum, yum!
Reader Seven: One jumped in the pool
Reader Eight: Where it was nice and cool.

Reader One: Two green frogs
Reader Two: Sat on a log
Reader Three: Eating the most
Reader Four: Delicious bugs.
Reader Five: Yum, yum, yum, yum.
Reader Six: Yum, yum, yum!
Reader Seven: One jumped in the pool
Reader Eight: Where it was nice and cool.

Reader One: One green frog
Reader Two: Sat on a log
Reader Three: Eating the most
Reader Four: Delicious bugs.
Reader Five: Yum, yum, yum, yum.
Reader Six: Yum, yum, yum!
Reader Seven: One jumped in the pool
Reader Eight: Where it was nice and cool.

Reader One: No green frogs
Reader Two: Sat on a log
Reader Three: Eating the most
Reader Four: Delicious bugs.
Reader Five: Yum, yum, yum, yum.
Reader Six: Yum, yum, yum!
Reader Seven: So I jumped in the pool!
Reader Eight: And it is nice and cool!

Three Blind Mice

Reader One: Three blind mice.

Reader Two: Three blind mice.

Reader Three: See how they run.

Reader Four: See how they run.

Reader Five: They all ran after the farmer's wife.

Reader Six: She cut off their tails with a carving knife.

Reader Seven: Did you ever see such a sight in your life?

Reader Eight: As three blind mice.

Reader One: Four fast mice.

Reader Two: Four fast mice.

Reader Three: See how they run.

Reader Four: See how they run.

Reader Five: They all ran after the farmer's cat.

Reader Six: The cat could not run. The cat was too fat.

Reader Seven: Did you ever see such a sight in your life?

Reader Eight: As four fast mice.

Reader One: Five fat mice.

Reader Two: Five fat mice.

Reader Three: See how they run.

Reader Four: See how they run.

Reader Five: They all ran after the farmer's dog.

Reader Six: He barked at the mice. They hid in a log.

Reader Seven: Did you ever see such a sight in your life?

Reader Eight: As five fat mice.

Reader One: Six scared mice.

Reader Two: Six scared mice.

Reader Three: See how they run.

Reader Four: See how they run.

Reader Five: They all ran after the farmer's horse.

Reader Six: He neighed at the mice. They ran home, of course.

Reader Seven: Did you ever see such a sight in your life?

Reader Eight: As six scared mice.

Reader One: Seven silly mice

Reader Two: Seven silly mice.

Reader Three: See how they run.

Reader Four: See how they run.

Reader Five: They all ran after the farmer's pig.

Reader Six: They played in the mud. They all danced a jig.

Reader Seven: Did you ever see such a sight in your life?

Reader Eight: As seven silly mice.

Reader One: Eight great mice

Reader Two: Eight great mice.

Reader Three: See how they run.

Reader Four: See how they run.

Reader Five: They all ran after the farmer's son.

Reader Six: He ran with the mice. He thought it was fun.

Reader Seven: Did you ever see such a sight in your life?

Reader Eight: As eight great mice.

Reader One: Nine fine mice.

Reader Two: Nine fine mice.

Reader Three: See how they run.

Reader Four: See how they run.

Reader Five: They all ran after the farmer's chick.

Reader Six: The chick ran back home. The mice were so quick.

Reader Seven: Did you ever see such a sight in your life?

Reader Eight: As nine fine mice.

Reader One: Ten tiny mice.

Reader Two: Ten tiny mice.

Reader Three: See how they run.

Reader Four: See how they run.

Reader Five: They all ran after the farmer's sheep.

Reader Six: The mice ran so hard. They all fell asleep.

Reader Seven: Did you ever see such a sight in your life?

Reader Eight: As ten tiny mice.

Chalk on the Walk

Reader One: Chalk on the walk.

Reader Two: Lots of things to do.

Reader Three: Chalk in lots of colors.

Reader Four: Let's do something new.

Reader Five: Red, pink, yellow, blue,

Reader Six: Green and purple, too.

Reader One: Names on the walk.

Reader Two: Yours and mine, too.

Reader Three: Names in lots of colors.

Reader Four: Let's do something new.

Reader Five: Red, pink, yellow, blue,

Reader Six: Green and purple, too.

Reader One: Shapes on the walk.

Reader Two: Triangles, squares, circles, too.

Reader Three: Shapes in lots of colors.

Reader Four: Let's do something new.

Reader Five: Red, pink, yellow, blue,

Reader Six: Green and purple, too.

Reader One: Pets on the walk.

Reader Two: Dogs, cats, kittens, too.

Reader Three: Pets in lots of colors.

Reader Four: Let's do something new.

Reader Five: Red, pink, yellow, blue,

Reader Six: Green and purple, too.

Reader One: Letters on the walk.

Reader Two: A, B, C and more to do.

Reader Three: Letters in lots of colors.

Reader Four: Let's do something new.

Reader Five: Red, pink, yellow, blue,

Reader Six: Green and purple, too.

Reader One: Numbers on the walk.

Reader Two: Five, four, three, and two.

Reader Three: Numbers in lots of colors.

Reader Four: Let's do something new.

Reader Five: Red, pink, yellow, blue,

Reader Six: Green and purple, too.

Reader One: Faces on the walk.

Reader Two: Mom and Dad, too.

Reader Three: Faces in lots of colors.

Reader Four: Let's do something new.

Reader Five: Red, pink, yellow, blue,

Reader Six: Green and purple, too.

Reader One: Flowers on the walk.

Reader Two: Roses, tulips too.

Reader Three: Chalk in lots of colors.

Reader Four: Let's do something new.

Reader Five: Red, pink, yellow, blue,

Reader Six: Green and purple, too.

Reader One: Rain on the walk.

Reader Two: What are we to do?

Reader Three: Rain washed off the colors.

Readers Four, Five, Six: We're all done. Are you?

Good Morning!

Reader One: Good morning! Good morning!

Reader Two: It's time to rise and shine.

Reader Three: Good morning! Good morning!

Reader Four: I hope you're feeling fine.

Reader Five: Good morning! Good morning!

Reader Six: Time to wake up, sleepyhead.

Reader Seven: Good morning! Good morning!

Reader Eight: Time to get up out of bed.

Reader Nine: Good morning! Good morning!

Reader Ten: It's time to rise and shine.

Reader Eleven: Good morning! Good morning!

Reader Twelve: I hope you're feeling fine.

Reader One: Good day! Good day!

Reader Two: It's time to go and play.

Reader Three: Good day! Good day!

Reader Four: I hope that you can stay.

Reader Five: Good day! Good day!

Reader Six: It's time to go back home.

Reader Seven: Good day! Good day!

Reader Eight: Now don't you go and roam.

Reader Nine: Good day! Good day!

Reader Ten: Please come again to play.

Reader Eleven: Good day! Good day!

Reader Twelve: I hope that you can stay.

Reader One: Good afternoon! Good afternoon!

Reader Two: It's time to set the table.

Reader Three: Good afternoon! Good afternoon!

Reader Four: Help me if you're able.

Reader Five: Good afternoon! Good afternoon!

Reader Six: It's time to have some lunch.

Reader Seven: Good afternoon! Good afternoon!

Reader Eight: I can hear you munch.

Reader Nine: Good afternoon! Good afternoon!

Reader Ten: It's time to clear the table.

Reader Eleven: Good afternoon! Good afternoon!

Reader Twelve: Help me if you're able.

Reader One: Good night! Good night!

Reader Two: It's time to go to bed.

Reader Three: Good night! Good night!

Reader Four: Time to rest your head.

Reader Five: Good night! Good night!

Reader Six: We hope your day was fine.

Reader Seven: Good night! Good night!

Reader Eight: Now please, don't you whine.

Reader Nine: Good night! Good night!

Reader Ten: It's time to go to bed.

Reader Eleven: Good night! Good night!

Reader Twelve: Time to rest your head.

Chapter Two

Animals

Animals have natural appeal for young students. The first verse of some of the scripts, such as "I Had a Little Hen" and "Six Little Ducks," may be familiar to some students. Some, such as "One Funny Bunny," can also be used to reinforce counting. The scripts and their accompanying teaching suggestions are in alphabetical order. For all the presentations, consider preparing simple costumes that can be worn over the students' clothes by purchasing a variety of extra large T-shirts in a variety of colors. A yellow T-shirt can represent a duck or a hen. Add face painting for instant costuming. The settings of a farm, pond, or forest can be depicted on a mural.

A Crow Is Black

Read through the script and ask students who Polly is. Discuss the four birds depicted in the script and compare how they are alike and different. Using chart paper or the chalkboard, create a grid and list the characteristics of each of the birds. Readers can wear shirts that correspond to the colors of the birds.

I Had a Little Hen

Read aloud the first verse. Ask the students if a hen could really wash, run errands, bake, and clean. Before reading the rest of the script, have the students speculate on what the following animals might do: cat, dog, guinea pig, parakeet, fish, horse. Compare their suggestions with the script. This script lends itself well to role-playing, and students may enjoy simple face painting to correspond to the animals. *Historical note:* In the seventeenth and eighteenth centuries, *hen* was likely used as a term of endearment, referring to a woman, thus making the verse more logical.

The Little Green Frog

Have one student practice leading the group, and eventually the audience, in saying the lines everyone speaks. Because the verses do not rely on rhyming, it is easy to have the students add verses. Consider changing the theme to vehicles for a new script.

Little Robin Redbreast

This rhythmical script describes a cat's efforts to catch a robin. Additional students can act out the roles of the robins and cat while the script is read aloud. A variation on the script could be developed with a squirrel being barked at by a dog.

One Funny Bunny

This script combines counting with rhyme, assonance, and alliteration. If preferred, the script can be read with one student reading the four lines associated with the individual animal. Alternatively, have one student read the lines for one funny bunny, two students read the lines for two fat cats, and so forth. Students can act out each of the animals. Prompt the audience that they are going to chime in with "Bye-bye" at the end.

Six Little Ducks

From ducks to cows, this familiar rhyme provides endless opportunities for additional verses. Students will quickly learn the pattern, making this easy to learn. Prompt the audience members to listen to the cues so that they can chime in on the last line of each verse. If preferred, have one student recite the lines for the entire animal's verse. Alternatively, have groups of six students recite each animal's lines in unison.

Snip Snap Turtle

This script uses onomatopoeia and alliteration for a rhythmic presentation of farm animals. The verses present a bit more challenge for readers; therefore, provide ample practice time. If preferred, have one student read all the lines for the turtle, followed by another student reading the next animal's lines. Students can act out each of the animals.

A Swarm of Bees in May

Enliven a study of insects with this humorous script. Some words, such as *swarm, moths, gnats,* may be unfamiliar. Allow ample practice time for students to prepare. Ask students to brainstorm other insects that might make them say "goodbye." Use new insects in the script, retaining the rest of the script as appropriate. For example, use mosquitoes in place of bees or ticks in place of fleas.

Three Young Rats

The individual lines in this script are more difficult than those in some other scripts. However, Readers One through Eleven read the same line repeatedly. The lines for Readers Twelve and Thirteen vary with each verse. Discuss the image evoked by such a zany appearance as described in the script.

Two Little Blackbirds

Students may be familiar with the fingerplay version of the first verse. If you wish to encourage audience participation, teach the movements to the students before starting the script. Substitute students' names if preferred.

Fingerplay instructions:

> Two little blackbirds (*Keep hands closed, with thumbs up for birds.*)
>
> Sitting on a hill.
>
> One was named Jack. (*Wiggle one thumb.*)
>
> The other named Jill. (*Wiggle the other thumb.*)
>
> Fly away Jack. (*Throw one hand over the shoulder.*)
>
> Fly away Jill. (*Throw one hand over the shoulder.*)
>
> Come back again Jack. (*Bring back one hand.*)
>
> Come back again Jill. (*Bring back the other hand.*)

Historical note: The first known recording of this fingerplay is from 1765 when Oliver Goldsmith, editor of *Mother Goose's Melody* (c. 1765), used stamp paper stuck on each index finger as he amused a young child. (Stamp paper: The cost of postage was determined by the distance traveled and the number of sheets of paper used. The first prepaid adhesive stamp, the Penny Black, was issue on May 6, 1840.)

A Crow Is Black

Reader One: A crow is black.
Reader Two: And Polly is green.
Reader Three: A duck is yellow.
Reader Four: And the owl isn't seen.

Reader One: The crow goes caw.
Reader Two: And Polly copies you.
Reader Three: A duck goes quack.
Reader Four: And the owl says "Who."

Reader One: A crow caws in the trees.
Reader Two: And Polly talks in her cage.
Reader Three: A duck quacks in the pond.
Reader Four: And the owl's tree is his stage.

Reader One: A crow's eyes are black.
Reader Two: And Polly has gray eyes.
Reader Three: A duck's eyes are brown.
Reader Four: And the owl's are black as he flies.

Reader One: The crow lives in a nest.
Reader Two: And Polly wishes she were free.
Reader Three: A duck sails on the water.
Reader Four: And the owl lives in the trees.

Reader One: A crow eats yellow corn.
Reader Two: And Polly chews on a cracker.
Reader Three: A duck eats fish and seeds.
Reader Four: And the owl's a good night tracker.

Reader One: The crow sleeps in its nest.
Reader Two: And Polly says "Night night."
Reader Three: A duck drifts on the water.
Reader Four: And the owl takes flight.

I Had a Little Hen

Reader One: I had a little hen,

Reader Two: The prettiest hen I've seen.

Reader Three: She washed up the dishes.

Reader Four: She kept the house clean.

Reader Five: She went to the mill

Reader Six: To fetch us some flour.

Reader Seven: And always got home

Reader Eight: In less than an hour.

Reader Nine: She baked me my bread.

Reader Ten: She brewed me my tea.

Reader Eleven: She sat by the fire.

Reader Twelve: And told a tale to me!

Reader One: I had a little cat,

Reader Two: The prettiest cat I've seen.

Reader Three: She chased out all the mice.

Reader Four: She kept the house clean.

Reader Five: She slept on the sill

Reader Six: In the summer sun.

Reader Seven: She always stayed home

Reader Eight: When her work was done.

Reader Nine: She sat on my lap.

Reader Ten: She purred very loud.

Reader Eleven: She never ran away.

Reader Twelve: And made me very proud!

Reader One: I had a little dog,

Reader Two: The prettiest dog I've seen.

Reader Three: She licked up all the spills.

Reader Four: To keep the house clean.

Reader Five: She barked to keep

Reader Six: All the strangers away.
Reader Seven: She always stayed home.
Reader Eight: She would never stray.
Reader Nine: She never bit me once.
Reader Ten: She was so very tame!
Reader Eleven: She loved to play ball.
Reader Twelve: It was her best game.

Reader One: I had a guinea pig,
Reader Two: The prettiest pig I've seen.
Reader Three: She made a little nest.
Reader Four: She kept her box clean.
Reader Five: She had lots of toys.
Reader Six: She used them to chew.
Reader Seven: She even chewed her ball.
Reader Eight: She chewed on me too!
Reader Nine: She was so very smart.
Reader Ten: Her coat was black and white.
Reader Eleven: I loved my guinea pig.
Reader Twelve: She was just right.

Reader One: I had a parakeet,
Reader Two: The prettiest bird I've seen.
Reader Three: She ate a lot of seeds.
Reader Four: She kept her cage clean.
Reader Five: She drank from her dish.
Reader Six: She sat on a swing.
Reader Seven: She played with her toys.
Reader Eight: She made her bell ring!
Reader Nine: She learned to say "hello."
Reader Ten: She was a pretty blue.
Reader Eleven: I loved my parakeet.
Reader Twelve: The sweetest bird I knew.

Reader One: I had a little fish,
Reader Two: The finest fish I've seen.
Reader Three: She ate a lot of food.
Reader Four: She kept her bowl clean.
Reader Five: She swam through the plants.
Reader Six: She swam all around.
Reader Seven: She swam to the top.
Reader Eight: Then she swam down.
Reader Nine: She couldn't really talk.
Reader Ten: She was a pretty gold.
Reader Eleven: I loved my little fish.
Reader Twelve: She lived 'til she was old.

Reader One: I want to have a horse,
Reader Two: The prettiest horse I've seen.
Reader Three: She would not cost a lot.
Reader Four: She would keep her stall clean.
Reader Five: She would eat lots of hay.
Reader Six: She would eat carrot sticks.
Reader Seven: She would give me a ride.
Reader Eight: She could learn lots of tricks!
Reader Nine: But my dad said no.
Reader Ten: Mom said no, too.
Reader Eleven: I have too many pets.
Reader Twelve: My room looks like a zoo!

The Little Green Frog

Reader One: Croak went the little green frog one day.
Reader Two: Croak went the little green frog.
Reader Three: Croak went the little green frog one day.
Reader Four: So we all went
Everyone: Croak! Croak! Croak!

Reader One: Ruff went the little black dog one day.
Reader Two: Ruff went the little black dog.
Reader Three: Ruff went the little black dog one day.
Reader Four: So we all went
Everyone: Ruff! Ruff! Ruff!

Reader One: Meow went the little white cat one day.
Reader Two: Meow went the little white cat.
Reader Three: Meow went the little white cat one day.
Reader Four: So we all went
Everyone: Meow! Meow! Meow!

Reader One: Tweet went the little blue bird one day.
Reader Two: Tweet went the little blue bird.
Reader Three: Tweet went the little blue bird one day.
Reader Four: So we all went
Everyone: Tweet! Tweet! Tweet!

Reader One: Moo went the little brown calf one day.
Reader Two: Moo went the little brown calf.
Reader Three: Moo went the little brown calf one day.
Reader Four: So we all went
Everyone: Moo! Moo! Moo!

Reader One: Hiss went the little green snake one day.
Reader Two: Hiss went the little green snake.
Reader Three: Hiss went the little green snake one day.
Reader Four: So we all went
Everyone: Hiss! Hiss! Hiss!

Reader One: Who said the little brown owl one day.
Reader Two: Who said the little brown owl.
Reader Three: Who said the little brown owl one day.
Reader Four: So we all went
Everyone: Who! Who! Who!

Reader One: Oink said the little pink pig one day.
Reader Two: Oink said the little pink pig.
Reader Three: Oink said the little pink pig one day.
Reader Four: So we all went
Everyone: Oink! Oink! Oink!

Reader One: Baa said the little white lamb one day.
Reader Two: Baa said the little white lamb.
Reader Three: Baa said the little white lamb one day.
Reader Four: So we all went
Everyone: Baa! Baa! Baa!

Reader One: Peep said the little yellow chick one day.
Reader Two: Peep said the little yellow chick.
Reader Three: Peep said the little yellow chick one day.
Reader Four: So we all went
Everyone: Peep! Peep! Peep!

Reader One: Maa said the little gray goat one day.
Reader Two: Maa said the little gray goat.
Reader Three: Maa said the little gray goat one day.
Reader Four: So we all went
Everyone: Maa! Maa! Maa!

Reader One: Quack said the little yellow duck one day.
Reader Two: Quack said the little yellow duck.
Reader Three: Quack said the little yellow duck one day.
Reader Four: So we all went
Everyone: Quack! Quack! Quack!

Reader One: Good night said the little farmer's wife one night.
Reader Two: Good night said the little farmer's wife.
Reader Three: Good night said the little farmer's wife one night.
Reader Four: So we all went
Everyone: Good night! Good night! Good night!

Little Robin Redbreast

Reader One: A little robin redbreast
Reader Two: Sat upon a tree,
Reader Three: Up went a cat,
Reader Four: And down went he!
Reader Five: Down came the cat,
Reader Six: And away the robin ran.
Reader Seven: Said the little robin,
Reader Eight: "Catch me if you can!"

Reader One: A little robin redbreast
Reader Two: Flew upon a wall,
Reader Three: A cat jumped after him,
Reader Four: And it began to call!
Reader Five: The little robin sang,
Reader Six: "What did you say?"
Reader Seven: The cat said, "Meow,"
Reader Eight: And the robin flew away.

Reader One: The little robin redbreast
Reader Two: Flew upon a house,
Reader Three: The cat looked at him,
Reader Four: And began to grouse!
Reader Five: The little robin sang,
Reader Six: "What did you say?"
Reader Seven: The cat said, "Come down here,"
Reader Eight: But the robin would not play.

Reader One: The little robin redbreast

Reader Two: Went to look for food.

Reader Three: He found a juicy worm.

Reader Four: He thought that it looked good.

Reader Five: The little robin ate it.

Reader Six: And went to look for more.

Reader Seven: The robin found a worm.

Reader Eight: And then he found four!

Reader One: The little robin redbreast

Reader Two: Didn't see the cat.

Reader Three: It sneaked up on the bird.

Reader Four: It tried to stay real flat.

Reader Five: A bigger robin came.

Reader Six: It was brown and gray.

Reader Seven: It flew at the cat.

Reader Eight: And scared the cat away.

Reader One: The little robin redbreast

Reader Two: Flew into its nest.

Reader Three: The bigger robin came.

Reader Four: And they both took a rest.

Reader Five: Both robins slept.

Reader Six: They didn't want to play.

Readers Seven: They both learned their lesson.

Reader Eight: They would not ever stray.

One Funny Bunny

Reader One: One funny bunny hops through the gate.

Reader Two: One funny bunny hops like it's late.

Reader Three: One funny bunny hops by the tree.

Reader Four: One funny bunny hops just like me.

Reader Five: Two fat cats nap on the bed.

Reader Six: Two fat cats love to be fed.

Reader Seven: Two fat cats purr on my knee.

Reader Eight: Two fat cats purr just like me.

Reader One: Three cute pups sit up and beg.

Reader Two: Three cute pups pull on my leg.

Reader Three: Three cute pups bark to be free.

Reader Four: Three cute pups bark just like me.

Reader Five: Four big birds wake up and sing.

Reader Six: Four big birds spread out their wings.

Reader Seven: Four big birds fly to the tree.

Reader Eight: Four big birds fly just like me.

Reader One: Five gray goats go for a walk.

Reader Two: Five gray goats climb up a rock.

Reader Three: Five gray goats climb high to see.

Reader Four: Five gray goats climb up like me.

Reader Five: Six fast fish swim up and down.

Reader Six: Six fast fish never can drown.

Reader Seven: Six fast fish swim in the sea.

Reader Eight: Six fast fish swim just like me.

Reader One: Seven black horses trot down the lane.
Reader Two: Seven black horses trot in the rain.
Reader Three: Seven black horses trot feeling free.
Reader Four: Seven black horses trot just like me.

Reader Five: Eight great moms talk to their sons.
Reader Six: Eight great moms talk just for fun.
Reader Seven: Eight great moms talk and drink tea.
Reader Eight: Eight great moms talk just like me.

Reader One: Nine fine dads run in the yard.
Reader Two: Nine fine dads run very hard.
Reader Three: Nine fine dads run from a bee.
Reader Four: Nine fine dads run just like me.

Reader Five: Ten big babies wake up and cry.
Reader Six: Ten big babies smile and say hi.
Reader Seven: Ten big babies giggle with glee.
Reader Eight: Ten big babies say bye just like me.

All Readers: Bye-bye!

Six Little Ducks

Reader One: Six little ducks
Reader Two: That I once knew.
Reader Three: Fat ones,
Reader Four: Skinny ones,
Reader Five: Fair ones, too.
Reader Six: But the one little duck
Reader Seven: With the feather on his back.
Reader Eight: He led the others
Reader Nine: With a quack, quack, quack.
Everyone: Quack, quack, quack.
Everyone: Quack, quack, quack.
Reader Ten: He led the others
Everyone: With a quack, quack, QUACK!

Reader One: Six little dogs
Reader Two: That I once knew.
Reader Three: Fat ones,
Reader Four: Skinny ones,
Reader Five: Fair ones too.
Reader Six: But the one little dog
Reader Seven: With the dark brown fur.
Reader Eight: He led the others
Reader Nine: With a grr, grr, grr.
Everyone: Grr, grr, grr.
Everyone: Grr, grr, grr.
Reader Ten: He led the others
Everyone: With a grr, grr, GRR!

Reader One: Six little kittens
Reader Two: That I once knew.
Reader Three: Fat ones,

Reader Four: Skinny ones,

Reader Five: Fair ones, too.

Reader Six: But the one little kitten

Reader Seven: With the yellow fur.

Reader Eight: He led the others

Reader Nine: With a purr, purr, purr.

Everyone: Purr, purr, purr.

Everyone: Purr, purr, purr.

Reader Ten: He led the others

Everyone: With a purr, purr, PURR!

Reader One: Six little wolves

Reader Two: That I once knew.

Reader Three: Fat ones,

Reader Four: Skinny ones,

Reader Five: Fair ones, too.

Reader Six: But the one little wolf

Reader Seven: That was on the prowl.

Reader Eight: He led the others

Reader Nine: With a howl, howl, howl.

Everyone: Howl, howl, howl.

Everyone: Howl, howl, howl.

Reader Ten: He led the others

Everyone: With a howl, howl, HOWL!

Reader One: Six little hens

Reader Two: That I once knew.

Reader Three: Fat ones,

Reader Four: Skinny ones,

Reader Five: Fair ones, too.

Reader Six: But the one little hen

Reader Seven: That looked like a duck.

Reader Eight: He led the others

Reader Nine: With a cluck, cluck, cluck.

Everyone: Cluck, cluck, cluck.

Everyone: Cluck, cluck, cluck.

Reader Ten: He led the others

Everyone: With a cluck, cluck, CLUCK!

Reader One: Six little lions

Reader Two: That I once knew.

Reader Three: Fat ones,

Reader Four: Skinny ones,

Reader Five: Fair ones, too.

Reader Six: But the one little lion

Reader Seven: Who was only four.

Reader Eight: He led the others

Reader Nine: With a roar, roar, roar.

Everyone: Roar, roar, roar.

Everyone: Roar, roar, roar.

Reader Ten: He led the others

Everyone: With a roar, roar, ROAR!

Reader One: Six little goats

Reader Two: That I once knew.

Reader Three: Fat ones,

Reader Four: Skinny ones,

Reader Five: Fair ones too.

Reader Six: But the one little goat

Reader Seven: Without a ma.

Reader Eight: He led the others

Reader Nine: With a baa, baa, baa.

Everyone: Baa, baa, baa.

Everyone: Baa, baa, baa.

Reader Ten: He led the others

Everyone: With a baa, baa, BAA!

Reader One: Six little ponies

Reader Two: That I once knew.

Reader Three: Fat ones,

Reader Four: Skinny ones,

Reader Five: Fair ones too.

Reader Six: But the one little pony

Reader Seven: That loved to eat hay.

Reader Eight: He led the others

Reader Nine: With a neigh, neigh, neigh.

Everyone: Neigh, neigh, neigh.

Everyone: Neigh, neigh, neigh.

Reader Ten: He led the others

Everyone: With a neigh, neigh, NEIGH!

Reader One: Six little cows

Reader Two: That I once knew.

Reader Three: Fat ones,

Reader Four: Skinny ones,

Reader Five: Fair ones too.

Reader Six: But the one little cow

Reader Seven: That loved to chew.

Reader Eight: He led the others

Reader Nine: With a moo, moo, moo.

Everyone: Moo, moo, moo.

Everyone: Moo, moo, moo.

Reader Ten: He led the others

Everyone: With a moo, moo, MOO!

Snip Snap Turtle

Reader One: Snip snap, snip snap, snip snap turtle.
Reader Two: Snip snap turtle.
Reader Three: Snip snap, snip snap turtle.
Reader Four: See the snapping turtle snap.
Reader Five: Then hide inside its shell.

Reader One: Yip yap, yip yap, yip yap pup.
Reader Two: Yip yap pup.
Reader Three: Yip yap, yip yap pup.
Reader Four: Hear the yipping puppy yap.
Reader Five: Then take a puppy nap.

Reader One: Purr hiss, purr hiss, purr hiss cat.
Reader Two: Purr hiss cat.
Reader Three: Purr hiss, purr hiss cat.
Reader Four: Hear the hissing cat play.
Reader Five: And scare the pup away.

Reader One: Trot prance, trot prance, trot prance horse.
Reader Two: Trot prance horse.
Reader Three: Trot prance, trot prance horse.
Reader Four: See the trotting horse prance.
Reader Five: He makes a happy dance.

Reader One: Hip hop, hip hop, hip hop bunny.
Reader Two: Hip hop bunny.
Reader Three: Hip hop, hip hop bunny.
Reader Four: See the bunny rabbit's tail.
Reader Five: He's hopping down the trail.

Reader One: Butt kick, butt kick, butt kick goat.

Reader Two: Butt kick goat.

Reader Three: Butt kick, butt kick goat.

Reader Four: See the butting goat kick.

Reader Five: Cans and pans and sticks.

Reader One: Hi bye, hi bye, hi bye parrot.

Reader Two: Hi bye parrot.

Reader Three: Hi bye, hi bye parrot.

Reader Four: In the morning he says hi.

Reader Five: At nighttime, he says bye.

Reader One: Ribbit hop, ribbit hop, ribbit hop frog.

Reader Two: Ribbit hop frog.

Reader Three: Ribbit hop, ribbit hop frog.

Reader Four: Hear the frog croak in the bog.

Reader Five: And hop upon the log.

Reader One: Moo low, moo low, moo low cow.

Reader Two: Moo low cow.

Reader Three: Moo low, moo low cow.

Reader Four: Hear the cow go moo, moo, moo.

Reader Five: It loves to chew, chew, chew.

Reader One: Goodbye, goodbye, goodbye friends.

Reader Two: Goodbye friends.

Reader Three: Goodbye, goodbye friends.

Reader Four: We like to share our farm with you.

Reader Five: We hope you like it too!

A Swarm of Bees in May

Reader One: A swarm of bees in May
Reader Two: Is worth a load of hay.
Reader Three: A swarm of bees in June
Reader Four: Is worth a silver spoon.
Reader Five: A swarm of bees in July
Reader Six: Buzz so very high.

Reader One: A swarm of fleas in May
Reader Two: Will make a big dog bay.
Reader Three: A swarm of fleas in June
Reader Four: Will make a big dog swoon.
Reader Five: A swarm of fleas in July
Reader Six: Will make a dog jump high.

Reader One: A swarm of moths in May
Reader Two: All look very gray.
Reader Three: A swarm of moths in June
Reader Four: All are gone by noon.
Reader Five: A swarm of moths in July
Reader Six: Will make a farmer cry.

Reader One: A swarm of ants in May
Reader Two: Why don't they go away?
Reader Three: A swarm of ants in June
Reader Four: Will be around at noon.
Reader Five: A swarm of ants in July
Reader Six: Always make me sigh.

Reader One: A swarm of bugs in May
Reader Two: Always make me sway.
Reader Three: A swarm of bugs in June
Reader Four: Sing a silly tune.
Reader Five: A swarm of bugs in July
Reader Six: Are always very spry.

Reader One: A swarm of gnats in May
Reader Two: Make me stay away.
Reader Three: A swarm of gnats in June
Reader Four: Always make me swoon.
Reader Five: A swarm of gnats in July
Reader Six: Always make me cry.

Reader One: A swarm of beetles in May
Reader Two: Make me want to stray.
Reader Three: A swarm of gnats in June
Reader Four: Cannot leave too soon.
Reader Five: A swarm of gnats in July
Reader Six: Make me say goodbye!

Three Young Rats

Reader One: Three young rats

Reader Two: With black felt hats.

Reader Three: Three young ducks

Reader Four: With white straw flats.

Reader Five: Three young dogs

Reader Six: With curling tails.

Reader Seven: Three young cats

Reader Eight: With white veils.

Reader Nine: Went out to walk

Reader Ten: With two young pigs

Reader Eleven: In satin vests and wigs.

Reader Twelve: But when it began to rain

Reader Thirteen: They all went home again.

Reader One: Three young rats

Reader Two: With black felt hats.

Reader Three: Three young ducks

Reader Four: With white straw flats.

Reader Five: Three young dogs

Reader Six: With curling tails.

Reader Seven: Three young cats

Reader Eight: With white veils.

Reader Nine: Went out to walk

Reader Ten: With two young pigs

Reader Eleven: In satin vests and wigs.

Reader Twelve: But when it began to thunder

Reader Thirteen: There was no place to run under.

Reader One: Three young rats
Reader Two: With black felt hats.
Reader Three: Three young ducks
Reader Four: With white straw flats.
Reader Five: Three young dogs
Reader Six: With curling tails.
Reader Seven: Three young cats
Reader Eight: With white veils.
Reader Nine: Went out to walk
Reader Ten: With two young pigs
Reader Eleven: In satin vests and wigs.
Reader Twelve: But when the wind began to blow
Reader Thirteen: They had to walk very slow.

Reader One: Three young rats
Reader Two: With black felt hats.
Reader Three: Three young ducks
Reader Four: With white straw flats.
Reader Five: Three young dogs
Reader Six: With curling tails.
Reader Seven: Three young cats
Reader Eight: With white veils.
Reader Nine: Went out to walk
Reader Ten: With two young pigs
Reader Eleven: In satin vests and wigs.
Reader Twelve: But when it began to snow
Reader Thirteen: Back home they did go.

Two Little Blackbirds

Reader One: Two little blackbirds

Reader Two: Sat upon a hill.

Reader Three: One was named Jack.

Reader Four: The other named Jill.

Reader Five: Fly away Jack.

Reader Six: Fly away Jill.

Reader Seven: Come back Jack.

Reader Eight: Come back Jill.

Reader One: There were two barn owls

Reader Two: Who sat in a tree.

Reader Three: One was named Raul.

Reader Four: The other named Bree.

Reader Five: Fly away Raul.

Reader Six: Fly away Bree.

Reader Seven: Come back Raul.

Reader Eight: Come back Bree.

Reader One: There were two green frogs

Reader Two: Who acted silly.

Reader Three: One was named Billy.

Reader Four: The other named Lilly.

Reader Five: Hop away Billy.

Reader Six: Hop away Lilly.

Reader Seven: Come back Billy.

Reader Eight: Come back Lilly.

Reader One: There were two fat dogs
Reader Two: Who chased my cat.
Reader Three: One was named Pete.
Reader Four: The other named Pat.
Reader Five: Run away Pete.
Reader Six: Run away Pat.
Reader Seven: Come back Pete.
Reader Eight: Come back Pat.

Reader One: There were two brown cows
Reader Two: That lived in a meadow.
Reader Three: One was named Nellie.
Reader Four: The other named Flo.
Reader Five: Go away Nellie.
Reader Six: Go away Flo.
Reader Seven: Come back Nellie.
Reader Eight: Come back Flo.

Reader One: There were two spotted ponies
Reader Two: That lived in the stall.
Reader Three: One was named Pat.
Reader Four: The other named Paul.
Reader Five: Run away Pat.
Reader Six: Run away Paul.
Reader Seven: Come back Pat.
Reader Eight: Come back Paul.

Reader One: There were two little kids
Reader Two: That lived in the house.
Reader Three: One was named Jen.
Reader Four: The other named Ben.
Reader Five: Go to sleep Jen.
Reader Six: Go to sleep Ben.
Reader Seven: Wake up Jen.
Reader Eight: Wake up Ben.

Chapter Three

Familiar Rhymes

Although well-known rhymes can be found in all the chapters, these scripts offer the best opportunity for capitalizing on familiar rhymes. Consider starting with common nursery rhymes, such as "Mary Had a Little Lamb" or "Three Little Kittens." If there is a preschool class in your school, have the students prepare a series of scripts to share with the younger students.

Dance with Your Daddy

This rhyme for babies offers predictability, rhythm, and repetition—all factors for instant success. Consider adding movement to the script by adding a swaying movement to lines one and three. Add the following gestures as preferred. Verse one: swimming motion for fish; verse two: hands on top of head for hat; verse three: wiggling fingers for ring; verse four: open hands for book; verse five: turning head for clock; verse six: lifting pretend cup to mouth for cup; verse seven: pointing to or lifting feet for shoes; verse eight: hands folded under tipped head for napping. *Historical note:* Commonly found as "Dance to Your Daddy," sung in Scotland in the early 1800s, this is also called a dandling song (holding up a baby and bouncing lightly while singing the song).

Hey Diddle Diddle

The pace of this variation, plus the harder words, will take some rehearsal. Discuss why this is sometimes called a nonsense rhyme—it doesn't make a lot of sense. However, the absurdity is what makes it fun. If preferred, the same five readers can read all the verses. *Historical note:* Recorded as early as the mid-1700s, it is possible that this poem is a satire of a scandal during the time of Queen Elizabeth. The cat is the queen and the dog is Robert Dudley, Earl of Leicester, whom she once referred to as her "lap dog." It is also speculated that the dish is a server at the royal court, whereas the spoon refers to a taste-tester. Another theory is that the rhyme refers to the constellations. None of the theories have been substantiated.

Jack Be Nimble

Once a group of students have learned this version, have the entire class learn it as a choral reading. On a day when the students are restless, have them stand up, recite the lines, and punctuate the end of each verse with a short hop. To help the students keep the verses straight, put the key words or pictures of key words on the board. (For example, draw a candle next to the number one, a drawing of wheat by number 2, and so forth.) *Historical note:* Candle jumping was popular in England, both as a sport and as a way of fortune-telling. This was especially popular in Buckinghamshire, where the lace makers would celebrate St. Catherine's Day by concluding the festivities with having the girls lift their skirts and jump over a burning candle. If the candle stayed lit, good luck in the forthcoming year was ensured.

Little Boy Blue

This script could be paired with scripts from the chapter with animal scripts. For gender balance, consider alternating *Little Boy...* with *Little Girl....* Have the students think about other ways to vary the script, such as *Big Boy Blue* or *Grandpa Blue. Historical note:* During the reign of King Henry VIII, Cardinal Thomas Wolsey, who had humble beginnings (the son of a butcher), largely ignored pressing religious affairs, earning criticism—and possibly inspiring this rhyme. Similarly, Charles II, while exiled in Paris, ignored the disarray in his country. See Chris Roberts's *Heavy Words Lightly Thrown* for more details surrounding this possible source for the rhyme.

Little Girl, Little Girl

This traditional nursery rhyme has an old-fashioned feel, and it will work well if presented with other traditional rhymes. If preferred, arrange the students in a call-and-response format, with Readers One, Two, Five, and Six on one side of the stage, with the balance on the other side. Have the group of readers turn slightly so that they are facing each other. *Historical note:* The reference in the first verse to the diamond likely refers to the crown jewels of England. Only the first verse is original; subsequent verses, if they existed, have been lost. This has been attributed to the times of both Queen Victoria and the Tudor Queen Elizabeth. The more commonly heard and related version is the following:

> Pussy cat, pussy cat, where have you been?
> I've been to London to look at the queen.
> Pussy cat, pussy cat, what did you there?
> I frightened a little mouse under her chair.

Little Miss Muffet

Before introducing this script, brainstorm a list of a variety of insects. Discuss which ones can be scary when encountered unexpectedly. Discuss how some insects, such as spiders, are helpful. Explain that a tuffet can be either an area of grass (from tuft of grass) or a low, three-legged stool. Whey is the watery part of milk that separates from the curds (cottage cheese) when making cheese. The last line was altered from the original (*And frightened Miss Muffet away*) to simplify the reading. If preferred, have reader five get up and run at the end, replacing Reader Five with a new one each time. *Historical note:* Miss Muffet may have been Patience Muffet, the daughter of Dr. Thomas Muffet, an entomologist who died in 1604. Variations have appeared, such as "Little Miss Mopsey, sat in the shopsey ...."

Mary Had a Little Lamb

This script may be familiar to many students. Coach the audience on repeating the second line in a call-and-response fashion. *Historical note:* The rhyme, scripted here in a slightly expanded form, was written in 1830 by Sarah Josepha Hale of Boston, based on a real incident that happened at a schoolhouse. Share with the students that having a lamb follow a child to school was not uncommon during this time in history. The first four lines were the first four lines of recorded speech. They are the words uttered by Thomas Edison into his new invention—the phonograph.

Mary, Mary, Quite Contrary

The first two lines of each verse are the same, providing your beginning readers with an easy task. Some of the variations have more challenging plant names. Discuss the words, noting that the plants are linked thematically. *Historical note:* Some historians link this first verse to Mary,

Queen of Scots, and her four ladies-in-waiting who were also named Mary. Others speculate that the rhyme refers to the persecution of Roman Church. Still others believe that it refers to dismay at the reinstatement of the Roman Church.

Miss Mary Mack

This is a variation on a clapping game, in which two children face each other, clapping in a pattern while chanting the rhyme. This script actively involves the audience. Practice the first four lines with the entire group to get the pattern. Create additional verses, if preferred. *Historical note:* In America, the children of slaves would chant the song while working in the fields.

Miss Polly Had a Dolly

This short script can be acted out with two students assuming the parts of the doctor and Miss Polly while the eight readers read the script. Have the students brainstorm what would bring the script to life, such as having Miss Polly holding a dolly and having the doctor carrying a toy medical kit or small black bag. Although no historical notes are available, this is a popular jump-rope song.

Rub a Dub Dub

The additional verses in the script provide inspiration for brainstorming more groups of people and animals to be in the tub. *Historical note:* Two variants on this English rhyme are mentioned in *The Oxford Dictionary of Nursery Rhymes,* edited by Iona and Peter Onie, p. 447. The earliest version, from the late 1700s, follows:

> Hey! rub-a-dub, ho! rub-a-dub, three maids in a tub,
> And who do you think were there?
> The butcher, the baker, the candlestick-maker,
> And all of them gone to the fair.

Three Little Kittens

This short script maintains the spirit of the rhyme but is arranged so that Readers One through Three read the kittens' part, with Readers Four through Six reading the mother's part. Alternatively, the audience can join in on the *meows. Historical note:* The original verses are credited to an English publisher, Addey, who had Eliza Follen (1787–1860), a New England writer of children's books, add them to her book, *New Nursery Songs for All Good Children.*

Dance with Your Daddy

Reader One: Dance with your daddy
Reader Two: My little baby.
Reader Three: Dance with your daddy
Reader Four: My little baby.
Reader Five: You shall have a fish
Reader Six: In a little dish.
Reader Seven: You shall have a fish
Reader Eight: When the boat comes in.

Reader One: Dance with your daddy
Reader Two: My little baby.
Reader Three: Dance with your daddy
Reader Four: My little baby.
Reader Five: You shall have a hat
Reader Six: For your little cat.
Reader Seven: You shall have a hat
Reader Eight: When the boat comes in.

Reader One: Dance with your daddy
Reader Two: My little baby.
Reader Three: Dance with your daddy
Reader Four: My little baby.
Reader Five: You shall have a ring
Reader Six: In the sunny spring.
Reader Seven: You shall have a ring
Reader Eight: When the boat comes in.

Reader One: Dance with your daddy
Reader Two: My little baby.
Reader Three: Dance with your daddy
Reader Four: My little baby.
Reader Five: You shall have a book
Reader Six: So you can take a look.
Reader Seven: You shall have a book
Reader Eight: When the boat comes in.

Reader One: Dance with your daddy
Reader Two: My little baby.
Reader Three: Dance with your daddy
Reader Four: My little baby.
Reader Five: You shall have a clock
Reader Six: That goes tick tock tick tock.
Reader Seven: You shall have a clock
Reader Eight: When the boat comes in.

Reader One: Dance with your daddy
Reader Two: My little baby.
Reader Three: Dance with your daddy
Reader Four: My little baby.
Reader Five: You shall have a cup
Reader Six: To drink your milk all up.
Reader Seven: You shall have a cup
Reader Eight: When the boat comes in.

Reader One: Dance with your daddy
Reader Two: My little baby.
Reader Three: Dance with your daddy
Reader Four: My little baby.
Reader Five: You shall have some shoes
Reader Six: And some socks that you can use.
Reader Seven: You shall have some shoes
Reader Eight: When the boat comes in.

Reader One: Dance with your daddy

Reader Two: My little baby.

Reader Three: Dance with your daddy

Reader Four: My little baby.

Reader Five: You will take a nap

Reader Six: On your daddy's lap.

Reader Seven: You shall take a nap

Reader Eight: When the boat comes in.

Hey Diddle Diddle

Reader One: Hey diddle, diddle.
Reader Two: The cat and the fiddle.
Reader Three: The cow jumped over the moon.
Reader Four: The little dog laughed to see such sport.
Reader Five: And the dish ran away with the spoon.

Reader Six: Hey toot, toot, toot.
Reader Seven: The fish and the flute.
Reader Eight: The turtle jumped over the dune.
Reader Nine: The fisherman laughed to see such sport.
Reader Ten: And the mermaid swam, singing a tune.

Reader One: Hey whoo, whoo, whoo.
Reader Two: The owl and the kazoo.
Reader Three: The squirrel jumped into the tree.
Reader Four: The little bat laughed to see such sport.
Reader Five: And the flea flew away with the bee.

Reader Six: Hey fingers and toes.
Reader Seven: The monkeys and pianos.
Reader Eight: The elephant swung on a vine.
Reader Nine: The zebra and snake laughed to see such sport.
Reader Ten: And the tiger sat down to dine.

Reader One: Hey thistle, thistle.
Reader Two: The dragon and whistle.
Reader Three: The unicorn sat in the lake.
Reader Four: The king and queen laughed to see such sport.
Reader Five: And the princess drank tea with her cake.

Reader Six: Hey brum, brum, brum.

Reader Seven: The octopus and drum.

Reader Eight: The whale swam through the sea.

Reader Nine: The shrimp and shark laughed to see such sport.

Reader Ten: And the crab said, "Tee hee hee."

Reader One: Hey blow, blow, blow.

Reader Two: The frog and oboe.

Reader Three: The bunny jumped down through a hole.

Reader Four: The prairie dog laughed to see such sport.

Reader Five: And the little fox went for a stroll.

Reader Six: Hush, hush, bye, bye

Reader Seven: The stars in the sky.

Reader Eight: Twinkled so high and so bright.

Reader Nine: The moon winked one eye to see such a sight.

Reader Ten: And said to the world, "Good night."

Jack Be Nimble

Reader One: Jack be nimble.
Reader Two: Jack be quick.
Reader Three: Jack jump over
Reader Four: The candlestick.

Reader Five: Jack be nimble.
Reader Six: Jack be fleet.
Reader Seven: Jack jump over
Reader Eight: The bundle of wheat.

Reader One: Jack be nimble.
Reader Two: Jack be quick.
Reader Three: Jack jump over
Reader Four: A pile of bricks.

Reader Five: Jack be nimble.
Reader Six: Jack be fast.
Reader Seven: Jack jump over
Reader Eight: A pile of grass.

Reader One: Jack be nimble.
Reader Two: Jack be quick.
Reader Three: Jack jump over
Reader Four: A flock of chicks.

Reader Five: Jack be nimble.
Reader Six: Jack be swift.
Reader Seven: Jack jump over
Reader Eight: The snow in a drift.

Reader One: Jack be nimble.
Reader Two: Jack be quick.
Reader Three: Jack roll over
Reader Four: And do a trick.

Reader Five: Jack is tired.
Reader Six: Jack is slow.
Reader Seven: Blow out the candle.
Reader Eight: It's time to go.

Little Boy Blue

Reader One: Little Boy Blue,

Reader Two: Come blow your horn,

Reader Three: The sheep's in the meadow,

Reader Four: The cow's in the corn.

Reader Five: Where is the little boy

Reader Six: That tends the sheep?

Reader Seven: He's under the haystack,

Reader Eight: Fast asleep.

Reader One: Little Boy Blue,

Reader Two: Come blow your horn,

Reader Three: The goose's in the meadow,

Reader Four: The pig's in the corn.

Reader Five: Where is the little boy

Reader Six: That tends the farm?

Reader Seven: He's under the haystack,

Reader Eight: Behind the barn.

Reader One: Little Boy Blue,

Reader Two: Come blow your horn,

Reader Three: The goat's in the meadow,

Reader Four: The elk's in the corn.

Reader Five: Where is the little boy

Reader Six: That tends the herd?

Reader Seven: He's under the haystack,

Reader Eight: Don't say a word.

Reader One: Little Boy Blue,

Reader Two: Come blow your horn,

Reader Three: The duck's in the meadow,

Reader Four: The chick's in the corn.

Reader Five: Where is the little boy

Reader Six: That tends the flock?

Reader Seven: He's under the haystack

Reader Eight: Asleep on a rock.

Reader One: Little Boy Blue,

Reader Two: Come blow your horn,

Reader Three: The colt's in the meadow,

Reader Four: The calf's in the corn

Reader Five: Where is the little boy

Reader Six: That tends the yard?

Reader Seven: He's under the haystack

Reader Eight: Sleeping hard.

Reader One: Little Boy Blue,

Reader Two: Come blow your horn,

Reader Three: The goat's in the meadow,

Reader Four: The dog's in the corn

Reader Five: Where is the little boy

Reader Six: That tends the dog's pup?

Reader Seven: He's under the haystack

Reader Eight: Let's wake him up!

(Audience applauds to wake him up.)

Little Girl, Little Girl

Reader One: Little girl, little girl
Reader Two: Where have you been?
Reader Three: I was picking roses
Reader Four: To give to the queen.
Reader Five: Little girl, little girl
Reader Six: What did she give you?
Reader Seven: She gave me a diamond
Reader Eight: As big as my shoe.

Reader One: Little girl, little girl
Reader Two: What did you bring?
Reader Three: I have some roses
Reader Four: To give to the king.
Reader Five: Little girl, little girl
Reader Six: What did he give you?
Reader Seven: He gave me a fur coat.
Reader Eight: It was brand new.

Reader One: Little girl, little girl
Reader Two: What did you spend?
Reader Three: I bought some roses
Reader Four: To give to my friend.
Reader Five: Little girl, little girl
Reader Six: What did she give you?
Reader Seven: She gave me a dolly
Reader Eight: All dressed in blue.

Reader One: Little girl, little girl

Reader Two: What is that plant?

Reader Three: I have a rose bush

Reader Four: To give to my aunt.

Reader Five: Little girl, little girl

Reader Six: What did she give you?

Reader Seven: She gave me a hug

Reader Eight: Not one, but two.

Reader One: Little girl, little girl

Reader Two: Have you been bad?

Reader Three: I was picking roses

Reader Four: To give to my dad.

Reader Five: Little girl, little girl

Reader Six: What did he give you?

Reader Seven: He gave me a dime.

Reader Eight: To spend at the zoo.

Reader One: Little girl, little girl

Reader Two: She sang tra la la.

Reader Three: She was picking roses.

Reader Four: To give to her ma.

Reader Five: Little girl, little girl

Reader Six: What did she give you?

Reader Seven: She gave me a kiss

Reader Eight: As sweet as the dew.

Little Miss Muffet

Reader One: Little Miss Muffet, sat on a tuffet,
Reader Two: Eating her curds and whey.
Reader Three: Along came a spider,
Reader Four: Who sat down beside her.
Reader Five: Miss Muffet ran away.

Reader One: Little Miss Muffet, came back to her tuffet,
Reader Two: To eat her curds and whey.
Reader Three: Along came a wasp,
Reader Four: Who flew right beside her!
Reader Five: Miss Muffet ran away.

Reader One: Little Miss Muffet, came back to her tuffet,
Reader Two: To eat her curds and whey.
Reader Three: Along came a cricket,
Reader Four: Who jumped right beside her!
Reader Five: Miss Muffet ran away.

Reader One: Little Miss Muffet, came back to her tuffet,
Reader Two: To eat her curds and whey.
Reader Three: Along came a bee,
Reader Four: Who buzzed right beside her.
Reader Five: Miss Muffet ran away.

Reader One: Little Miss Muffet, came back to her tuffet,
Reader Two: To eat her curds and whey.
Reader Three: Along came a stink bug,
Reader Four: Who fell right on her.
Reader Five: Miss Muffet ran away.

Reader One: Little Miss Muffet, came back to her tuffet,
Reader Two: To eat her curds and whey.
Reader Three: Along came a slug,
Reader Four: Who slid right by her.
Reader Five: Miss Muffet ran away.

Reader One: Little Miss Muffet, came back to her tuffet,
Reader Two: To eat her curds and whey.
Reader Three: Along came a butterfly,
Reader Four: Who sat down beside her.
Reader Five: Miss Muffet decided to stay.

Mary Had a Little Lamb

Reader One: Mary had a little lamb,
Reader Two: Little lamb,
Everyone: Little lamb.
Reader Three: Mary had a little lamb,
Reader Four: Its fleece was white as snow.

Reader One: Everywhere that Mary went,
Reader Two: Mary went,
Everyone: Mary went.
Reader Three: Everywhere that Mary went,
Reader Four: The lamb was sure to go.

Reader One: It followed her to school one day,
Reader Two: School one day,
Everyone: School one day.
Reader Three: It followed her to school one day,
Reader Four: Which was against the rules.

Reader One: It made the children laugh and play,
Reader Two: Laugh and play,
Everyone: Laugh and play.
Reader Three: It made the children laugh and play,
Reader Four: To see a lamb at school.

Reader One: The teacher sent the lamb away,
Reader Two: Lamb away.
Everyone: Lamb away.
Reader Three: The teacher sent the lamb away,
Reader Four: But the lamb would not go.

Reader One: The lamb waited by the door,
Reader Two: By the door,
Everyone: By the door.
Reader Three: The lamb waited by the door,
Reader Four: 'Til Mary left for home.

Reader One: Why does the lamb love Mary so,
Reader Two: Love Mary so,
Everyone: Love Mary so?
Reader Three: "Why does the lamb love Mary so,
Reader Four: All the children cried.

Reader One: Why, Mary loves the little lamb
Reader Two: Little lamb,
Everyone: Little lamb.
Reader Three: Why, Mary loves the little lamb,
Reader Four: The teacher did reply.

Mary, Mary, Quite Contrary

Reader One: Mary, Mary quite contrary
Reader Two: How does your garden grow?
Reader Three: With silver bells and cockleshells
Reader Four: And pretty maids all in a row.

Reader One: Mary, Mary quite contrary
Reader Two: How does your garden grow?
Reader Three: With Queen Ann's lace and baby's breath
Reader Four: And sweet peas all in a row.

Reader One: Mary, Mary quite contrary
Reader Two: How does your garden grow?
Reader Three: With kangaroo's paw and lobster's claw
Reader Four: And lamb's ear all in a row.

Reader One: Mary, Mary quite contrary
Reader Two: How does your garden grow?
Reader Three: With turtle head and snake head
Reader Four: And mouse ear all in a row.

Reader One: Mary, Mary quite contrary
Reader Two: How does your garden grow?
Reader Three: With lemon balm and orange blossom
Reader Four: And lime fruit all in a row.

Reader One: Mary, Mary quite contrary
Reader Two: How does your garden grow?
Reader Three: With allspice and rosemary
Reader Four: And basil all in a row.

Reader One: Mary, Mary quite contrary
Reader Two: How does your garden grow?

Reader Three: With unicorn root and dragon's blood
Reader Four: And snapdragons all in a row.

Reader One: Mary, Mary quite contrary
Reader Two: How does your garden grow?
Reader Three: With raspberry and blueberry
Reader Four: And strawberry all in a row.

Reader One: Mary, Mary quite contrary
Reader Two: How does your garden grow?
Reader Three: With sea fennel and sea lavender
Reader Four: And seaweed all in a row.

Reader One: Mary, Mary quite contrary
Reader Two: How does your garden grow?
Reader Three: With peach trees and apricot trees
Reader Four: And apple trees all in a row.

Reader One: Mary, Mary quite contrary
Reader Two: How does your garden grow?
Reader Three: With horsemint and mare's tail
Reader Four: And horseradish all in a row.

Reader One: Mary, Mary quite contrary
Reader Two: How does your garden grow?
Reader Three: With kidneywort and liverwort
Reader Four: And lungwort all in a row.

Reader One: Mary, Mary quite contrary
Reader Two: How does your garden grow?
Reader Three: With dogwood and hound's tongue
Reader Four: And fleabane all in a row.

Reader One: Mary, Mary quite contrary
Reader Two: How does your garden grow?
Reader Three: With catnip and catmint
Reader Four: And catsfoot all in a row.

Miss Mary Mack

Reader One: Miss Mary Mack,

Everyone: Mack, Mack.

Reader Two: All dressed in black,

Everyone: Black, black.

Reader Three: With silver buttons,

Everyone: Buttons, buttons.

Reader Four: All down her back,

Everyone: Back, back.

Reader Five: She asked her mother,

Everyone: Mother, mother.

Reader Six: For fifteen cents,

Everyone: Cents, cents.

Reader Seven: To see the elephants,

Everyone: Elephants, elephants.

Reader Eight: Jump over the fence,

Everyone: Fence, fence.

Reader Nine: They jumped so high,

Everyone: High, high.

Reader Ten: They reached the sky,

Everyone: Sky, sky.

Reader Eleven: And they never came back,

Everyone: Back, back.

Reader Twelve: 'Til the fourth of July,

Everyone: July, July.

Reader One: Miss Mary Mack,

Everyone: Mack, Mack.

Reader Two: All dressed in black,

Everyone: Black, black.

Reader Three: With silver buttons,

Everyone: Buttons, buttons.

Reader Four: All down her back,

Everyone: Back, back.

Reader Five: She asked her mother,

Everyone: Mother, mother.

Reader Six: For fifteen cents,

Everyone: Cents, cents.

Reader Seven: To see the monkeys,

Everyone: Monkeys, monkeys.

Reader Eight: Grab all the hats,

Everyone: Hats, hats.

Reader Nine: They piled them so high,

Everyone: High, high.

Reader Ten: They reached the sky,

Everyone: Sky, sky.

Reader Eleven: And they never fell down,

Everyone: Down, down.

Reader Twelve: Till they took the queen's crown,

Everyone: Crown, crown.

Reader One: Miss Mary Mack,

Everyone: Mack, Mack.

Reader Two: All dressed in black,

Everyone: Black, black.

Reader Three: With silver buttons,

Everyone: Buttons, buttons.

Reader Four: All down her back,

Everyone: Back, back.

Reader Five: She asked her mother,

Everyone: Mother, mother.

Reader Six: For fifteen cents,

Everyone: Cents, cents.

Reader Seven: To see the clowns,

Everyone: Clowns, clowns.

Reader Eight: Bounce around in the tent,

Everyone: Tent, tent.

Reader Nine: They bounced so high,

Everyone: High, high.

Reader Ten: They reached the top,

Everyone: Top, top.

Reader Eleven: And they never came down,

Everyone: Down, down.

Reader Twelve: Till the circus left the town,

Everyone: Town, town.

Miss Polly Had a Dolly

Reader One: Miss Polly had a dolly.

Reader Two: She was sick, sick, sick.

Reader Three: Polly called for the doctor.

Reader Four: "Come quick, quick, quick."

Reader Five: The doctor came

Reader Six: With his bag and his hat.

Reader Seven: He knocked on the door

Reader Eight: With a rat-a-tat-tat.

Reader One: He looked at the dolly.

Reader Two: He shook his head.

Reader Three: Then he said,

Reader Four: "Polly, put her to bed."

Reader Five: He gave Polly a pill.

Reader Six: And then he said,

Reader Seven: "I'll be back in the morning

Reader Eight: If she's still ill, ill, ill."

Reader One: Miss Polly had a dolly.

Reader Two: She was sick, sick, sick.

Reader Three: She gave her a pill.

Reader Four: It worked quick, quick, quick.

Reader Five: Polly called the doctor

Reader Six: And she said,

Reader Seven: "My dolly's not sick.

Reader Eight: The pill did the trick, trick, trick."

Reader One: Miss Polly had a dolly

Reader Two: She was well, well, well.

Reader Three: The doctor came back

Reader Four: And rang the bell, bell, bell.

Reader Five: Polly said to the doctor

Reader Six: "My dolly's not ill."

Reader Seven: "I know," said the doctor.

Reader Eight: "Here's my bill, bill, bill."

Rub a Dub Dub

All Readers: Rub a dub dub.

Reader One: Three men in a tub.

Reader Two: And who do you think they be?

Reader Three: The butcher, the baker,

Reader Four: The candlestick maker.

Reader Five: Turn them about, all three.

All Readers: Rub a dub dub.

Reader One: Three women in a tub.

Reader Two: And who do you think they be?

Reader Three: The writer, the singer,

Reader Four: The church bell ringer.

Reader Five: Turn them about, all three.

All Readers: Rub a dub dub.

Reader One: Three kids in a tub.

Reader Two: And who do you think they be?

Reader Three: The sister, the brother,

Reader Four: The babe without mother.

Reader Five: Turn them about, all three.

All Readers: Rub a dub dub.

Reader One: Three musicians in a tub.

Reader Two: And who do you think they be?

Reader Three: The piper, the drummer,

Reader Four: The banjo strummer.

Reader Five: Turn them about, all three.

All Readers: Rub a dub dub.

Reader One: Three dogs in a tub.

Reader Two: And who do you think they be?

Reader Three: The puppy, the hound,

Reader Four: The pooch from the pound.

Reader Five: Turn them about, all three.

All Readers: Rub a dub dub.

Reader One: Three bugs in a tub.

Reader Two: And who do you think they be?

Reader Three: The fly, the bee,

Reader Four: The puppy dog's flea

Reader Five: Turn them about, all three.

All Readers: Rub a dub dub.

Reader One: Three cats in a tub.

Reader Two: And who do you think they be?

Reader Three: The kitten, the tabby,

Reader Four: The tomcat that's crabby.

Reader Five: Turn them about, all three.

All Readers: Rub a dub dub.

Reader One: Three fish in a tub.

Reader Two: And who do you think they be?

Reader Three: The tuna, the cod,

Reader Four: The whale from a pod.

Reader Five: Turn them about, all three.

All Readers: Rub a dub dub.

Reader One: There's a hole in the tub.

Reader Two: And where do you think they be?

Reader Three: The people, the animals,

Reader Four: Bugs, fish, and all.

Reader Five: Turned out and into the sea.

Three Little Kittens

Reader One: Three little kittens
Reader Two: Have lost their mittens.
Reader Three: And they began to cry
Readers One, Two Three: Meow, meow, meow.

Reader Four: Oh, my, little kittens
Reader Five: Where are your mittens?
Reader Six: And why do you all cry?
Readers One, Two Three: Meow, meow, meow.

Reader One: Oh, Mother dear,
Reader Two: We sadly fear,
Reader Three: Our mittens they are lost.
Readers One, Two Three: Meow, meow, meow.

Reader Four: What? Lost your mittens!
Reader Five: You poor little kittens.
Reader Six: Now you will really cry.
Readers One, Two Three: Meow, meow, meow.

Reader Four: Such bad little kittens
Reader Five: To lose your mittens!
Reader Six: You shall have no pie.
Readers One, Two Three: Meow, meow, meow.

Reader One: No pie, cried the kittens!
Reader Two: We must find our mittens.
Reader Three: We must have some pie.
Readers One, Two Three: Meow, meow, meow.

Reader One: Mother, dear. Come here. Come here.
Reader Two: We have found our mittens.
Reader Three: Can we have some pie?
Readers One, Two Three: Meow, meow, meow.

Reader Four: Found your mittens!

Reader Five: You are such good kittens.

Reader Six: Now you don't have to cry.

Readers One, Two Three: Meow, meow, meow.

Reader Four: Come in the house.

Reader Five: Take off those mittens.

Reader Six: Then you shall have your pie.

Readers One, Two Three: Meow, meow, meow.

Reader One: The three little kittens

Reader Two: Did *not* take off their mittens.

Reader Three: Then they began to cry.

Readers One, Two Three: Meow, meow, meow.

Reader One: Oh! Mother dear,

Reader Two: We greatly fear.

Reader Three: That we have soiled our mittens.

Readers One, Two Three: Meow, meow, meow.

Reader Four: What? Soiled your mittens?

Reader Five: You naughty kittens!

Reader Six: And they all began to cry.

Readers One, Two Three: Meow, meow, meow.

Reader One: The three little kittens

Reader Two: Washed their mittens

Reader Three: And hung them out to dry.

Readers One, Two Three: Meow, meow, meow.

Reader One: Oh! Mother dear,

Reader Two: Do you not hear?

Reader Three: That we have washed our mittens.

Readers One, Two Three: Meow, meow, meow.

Reader Four: What? Washed your mittens?

Reader Five: You good little kittens!

Reader Six: But I smell a rat close by!

Readers One, Two Three: Meow, meow, meow.

Everyone: We smell a rat close by!

Chapter Four

Family, Friends, Feelings, and Fun

These five scripts are less familiar than many of those found in preceding chapters. Incorporate these scripts into units on family or when discussing the importance of being good to friends. The repetition and rhyme offer opportunities for additional verses.

I Have a Little Sister

This script can be revised or expanded to include the names of the students and their favorite activities, plus their family members, friends, and pets. Encourage the creation of new verses, even if they don't rhyme. *Historical note:* This was liberally adapted from the following riddle from the 1800s:

I have a little sister, they call her Peep-Peep,
She wades in the waters, deep, deep, deep;
She climbs the mountains high, high, high;
Poor little creature she has but one eye.

Answer: A star.

There Are Smiles

Before reading aloud this script, brainstorm all the reasons people smile. If the students struggle with suggestions, identify times you've seen the students smile and discuss the reasons behind the smiles. After learning the script, ask students if they can think of other kinds of smiles. To enliven the presentation, selected students could pantomime the various activities that are prompting the smiles (greeting friends, saying "I love you," and the like).

There Was a Family

Introduce this script about family members by reading aloud or writing the first two lines of a verse on the board: *There was a mother who loved to bake bread.* Ask the children to suggest words that rhyme with *bread.* Create their couplet and then compare it with the script. Continue with other verses in like fashion. Compare the class's version with this one, discussing how authors can make very different choices.

What Do You Do to Have Fun?

Introduce the script by exploring what the class does in each of the situations posed (things to do to have fun, on rainy days, on the first day of school, and the like). This script poses the question, exploring it in eight lines. The answer follows in the next set of eight lines. If preferred, have two sets of readers, with the second set answering the questions.

When You've Been Sad

Consider pairing this script with *There Are Smiles.* Introduce the script by discussing times when you've felt bad, lonely, or regretful. Talk about what you do to feel better. Ask the students to talk about things they do. Then read aloud the verses and discuss how the advice is always to go home. Be sensitive to those situations or settings for which home may not be the safest place, omitting this script if it might prove to be uncomfortable for individuals.

I Have a Little Sister

Reader One: I have a little sister.

Reader Two: Named Peep, Peep, Peep.

Reader Three: She wades in the waters,

Reader Four: Deep, deep, deep.

Reader Five: She climbs the mountains

Reader Six: High, high, high.

Reader Seven: To get up to the

Reader Eight: Sky, sky, sky.

Reader One: I have a little brother.

Reader Two: Named Jim, Jim, Jim

Reader Three: He goes climbing at the

Reader Four: Gym, gym, gym.

Reader Five: He climbs the walls

Reader Six: Up, up, up

Reader Seven: To win the gold

Reader Eight: Cup, cup, cup.

Reader One: I have a father.

Reader Two: Named Jay, Jay, Jay

Reader Three: He works hard at the office all

Reader Four: Day, day, day.

Reader Five: He plays baseball with a

Reader Six: Bat, bat, bat

Reader Seven: He wears a blue and yellow

Reader Eight: Hat, hat, hat.

Reader One: I have a mother.

Reader Two: Named May, May, May

Reader Three: She works hard at home all

Reader Four: Day, day, day.

Reader Five: She bakes us cookies and
Reader Six: Cakes, cakes, cakes.
Reader Seven: She never takes a
Reader Eight: Break, break, break.

Reader One: I have a grandfather.
Reader Two: Named Gramps, Gramps, Gramps.
Reader Three: He really loves to
Reader Four: Camp, camp, camp.
Reader Five: We get to sleep in a
Reader Six: Tent, tent, tent.
Reader Seven: That's how our summers are
Reader Eight: Spent, spent, spent.

Reader One: I have a grandmother.
Reader Two: Named Gran, Gran, Gran.
Reader Three: She makes fudge in a
Reader Four: Pan, pan, pan.
Reader Five: All that she makes is
Reader Six: Sweet, sweet, sweet.
Reader Seven: Then we help her
Reader Eight: Eat, eat, eat.

Reader One: My name is Kate.
Reader Two: I'm eight, eight, eight.
Reader Three: I really love to
Reader Four: Skate, skate, skate.
Reader Five: My family loves to
Reader Six: Play, play, play.
Reader Seven: We try to play every
Reader Eight: Day, day, day.

There Are Smiles

Reader One: There are smiles that make us happy.

Reader Two: When our friends we see.

Reader Three: There are smiles that make us happy.

Reader Four: Just being you and me.

Reader One: There are smiles that say I love you.

Reader Two: When Mom and Dad see you.

Reader Three: There are smiles that say I love you.

Reader Four: Just between us, too.

Reader One: There are smiles that are big.

Reader Two: When you are feeling proud.

Reader Three: There are smiles that are big.

Reader Four: They make you laugh out loud.

Reader One: There are smiles that are special.

Reader Two: Between a friend or two.

Reader Three: There are smiles that are special.

Reader Four: Just between us, too.

Reader One: There are smiles that make us laugh.

Reader Two: At funny things we do.

Reader Three: There are smiles that make us laugh.

Reader Four: Just being me and you.

Reader One: There are smiles that make us blue.

Reader Two: When we say goodbye.

Reader Three: There are smiles that make us blue.

Reader Four: And we want to cry.

Reader One: There are smiles that are silly.
Reader Two: After some things that we do.
Reader Three: There are smiles that are silly.
Reader Four: Just being me and you.

Reader One: There are smiles that are dreamy.
Reader Two: When you see a shooting star.
Reader Three: There are smiles that are dreamy.
Reader Four: When the star is from afar.

Reader One: There are smiles that are sweet.
Reader Two: When you get a treat.
Reader Three: There are smiles that are sweet.
Reader Four: When the treat is sweet to eat.

Reader One: There are smiles that are bright.
Reader Two: When you get a surprise.
Reader Three: There are smiles that are bright.
Reader Four: That smile is a prize.

Reader One: There are smiles that bring me sunshine.
Reader Two: They are the smiles that you give to me.
Reader Three: Do my smiles bring you sunshine?
Reader Four: The best smiles are all free.

There Was a Family

Reader One: There was a mother
Reader Two: Who loved to make bread.
Reader Three: She'd feed all her kids
Reader Four: And put them to bed.

Reader One: There was a brother
Reader Two: Who ran so fast.
Reader Three: He ran a race.
Reader Four: He was not last.

Reader One: There was a grandma
Reader Two: Who liked to knit.
Reader Three: She liked a warm fire.
Reader Four: There she would sit.

Reader One: There was a grandpa
Reader Two: Who went to Spain.
Reader Three: Then he returned
Reader Four: And went there again.

Reader One: There was a sister
Reader Two: Who went out to play.
Reader Three: Then she came home
Reader Four: She came home to stay.

Reader One: There was a dad
Reader Two: Who was so tall.
Reader Three: He'd call to his son
Reader Four: So they could play ball.

Reader One: There was a cat
Reader Two: Who climbed up a tree.
Reader Three: Then he came down
Reader Four: One, two, three.

Reader One: There was a crow
Reader Two: Who sat on a stone.
Reader Three: When he was gone
Reader Four: Then there was none.

Reader One: There was a horse
Reader Two: Who was going to the mill.
Reader Three: He was a stung by a bee.
Reader Four: He did not stand still.

Reader One: There was a butcher
Reader Two: Who cut up meat.
Reader Three: He stood all day
Reader Four: Upon his feet.

Reader One: There was a dog
Reader Two: Who ran after sticks.
Reader Three: He'd sit up and beg
Reader Four: And do other tricks.

Reader One: There was a cobbler
Reader Two: Who could fix shoes.
Reader Three: When they were mended
Reader Four: He took a snooze.

Reader One: That is my family.
Reader Two: They are all mine.
Reader Three: And as you have seen.
Reader Four: They are so fine!

What Do You Do to Have Fun?

Reader One: What do you do to have fun?
Reader Two: When you play outside in the sun?
Reader Three: Do you ride a bike,
Reader Four: Fly a kite,
Reader Five: Or take a hike?
Reader Six: Do you swing on a swing?
Reader Seven: Do you do some other thing?
Reader Eight: What do you do to have fun?

Reader One: Here's what I do to have fun
Reader Two: When I play outside in the sun.
Reader Three: I ride my bike.
Reader Four: I fly a kite.
Reader Five: Or I take a hike.
Reader Six: I swing on my swing.
Reader Seven: And I do other things.
Reader Eight: That's what I do to have fun.

Reader One: What do you do on rainy days?
Reader Two: When you can't go outside to play?
Reader Three: Do you color with red, white, and blue?
Reader Four: Do you paint with your fingers, too?
Reader Five: Do you cut and paste and glue?
Reader Six: Do you read great books with your friends?
Reader Seven: Do you wish that the rain wouldn't end?
Reader Eight: What do you do on rainy days?

Reader One: Here's what I on rainy days

Reader Two: When I can't go outside to play.

Reader Three: I color with red, white, and blue.

Reader Four: I paint with my fingers, too.

Reader Five: I cut and paste and glue.

Reader Six: I read great books with my friends.

Reader Seven: I wish that the rain wouldn't end.

Reader Eight: That's what I do on rainy days.

Reader One: What do you do on the first day of school?

Reader Two: When you can't go swim in the pool?

Reader Three: Do you put on new clothes with no muss?

Reader Four: Do you get on a big yellow bus?

Reader Five: Do you line up at the school with no fuss?

Reader Six: Do you learn new words you can spell?

Reader Seven: Do you go out to recess and yell?

Reader Eight: What do you do on the first day of school?

Reader One: Here's what I do on the first day of school

Reader Two: When I can't go swim in the pool.

Reader Three: I put on new clothes with no muss.

Reader Four: I get on a big yellow bus.

Reader Five: I line up at the school with no fuss.

Reader Six: I learn new words I can spell.

Reader Seven: I go out to recess, but don't yell.

Reader Eight: That's what I do on the first day of school.

Reader One: What do you do on your birthday?

Reader Two: When you wake up and say "It's today!"

Reader Three: Do you greet the day with a smile?

Reader Four: Do you hope it will last quite a while?

Reader Five: Do you look at your gifts in a pile?

Reader Six: Do you pick up a present to shake?

Reader Seven: Do you eat some ice cream and cake?

Reader Eight: What do you do on your birthday?

Reader One: Here's what I do on my birthday.

Reader Two: When I wake up, I say, "It's today!"

Reader Three: I greet the day with a smile.

Reader Four: I hope it will last quite a while.

Reader Five: I look at my gifts in a pile.

Reader Six: I pick up a present to shake.

Reader Seven: We all eat some ice cream and cake.

Reader Eight: That's what I do on my birthday.

Reader One: What do you do when it's night?

Reader Two: When the stars and the moon are so bright?

Reader Three: Do you ask to stay up, beg and plead?

Reader Four: Do you find a good book you can read?

Reader Five: Do you ask for snacks that you really need?

Reader Six: Do you snuggle down deep in your bed?

Reader Seven: Do you get kissed goodnight on your head?

Reader Eight: What do you do when it's night?

Reader One: Here's what I do when it's night.

Reader Two: I wish on a star that is bright.

Reader Three: I ask to stay up, beg and plead.

Reader Four: Then I find a good book I can read.

Reader Five: I ask for some snacks that I need.

Reader Six: Then I snuggle down deep in my bed.

Reader Seven: I get kissed goodnight on my head.

Reader Eight: That's what I do when it's night.

When You've Been Sad

Reader One: When you've been sad,
Reader Two: Where will you run to?
Reader Three: When you've been sad,
Reader Four: Where will you run to?
Reader Five: Run to the moon,
Reader Six: Oh moon, won't you hide me?
Reader Seven: Run to the moon,
Reader Eight: Oh moon, won't you hide me?
Reader Nine: No, said the moon,
Reader Ten: I won't hide you.
Reader Eleven: You must go home.

Reader One: When you've been silly,
Reader Two: Where will you run to?
Reader Three: When you've been silly,
Reader Four: Where will you run to?
Reader Five: Run to the stars,
Reader Six: Oh stars, won't you hide me?
Reader Seven: Run to the stars,
Reader Eight: Oh stars, won't you hide me?
Reader Nine: No, said the stars.
Reader Ten: We won't hide you.
Reader Eleven: You must go home.

Reader One: When you've been tired,
Reader Two: Where will you run to?
Reader Three: When you've been tired,
Reader Four: Where will you run to?
Reader Five: Run to the breeze,

Reader Six: Oh breeze, won't you hide me?

Reader Seven: Run to the breeze,

Reader Eight: Oh breeze, won't you hide me?

Reader Nine: No, said the breeze.

Reader Ten: I won't hide you.

Reader Eleven: You must go home.

Reader One: When you've been hurt,

Reader Two: Where will you run to?

Reader Three: When you've been hurt,

Reader Four: Where will you run to?

Reader Five: Run to the sea,

Reader Six: Oh sea, won't you hide me?

Reader Seven: Run to the sea,

Reader Eight: Oh sea, won't you hide me?

Reader Nine: No, said the sea.

Reader Ten: I won't hide you.

Reader Eleven: You must go home.

Reader One: When you've been sorry,

Reader Two: Where will you to?

Reader Three: When you've been sorry,

Reader Four: Where will you run to?

Reader Five: Run to the rocks,

Reader Six: Oh rocks, won't you hide me?

Reader Seven: Run to the rocks,

Reader Eight: Oh rocks, won't you hide me?

Reader Nine: No, said the rocks.

Reader Ten: We won't hide you.

Reader Eleven: You must go home.

Reader One: When you've been careless,
Reader Two: Where will you run to?
Reader Three: When you've been careless,
Reader Four: Where will you run to?
Reader Five: Run to the trees,
Reader Six: Oh trees, won't you hide me?
Reader Seven: Run to the trees,
Reader Eight: Oh trees, won't you hide me?
Reader Nine: No, said the trees.
Reader Ten: We won't hide you.
Reader Eleven: You must go home.

Reader One: When you've been bad,
Reader Two: Where will you run to?
Reader Three: When you've been bad,
Reader Four: Where will you run to?
Reader Five: I guess I'll stay home,
Reader Six: And face the music.
Reader Seven: I guess I'll stay home,
Reader Eight: And face the music.
Reader Nine: I guess I'll stay home,
Reader Ten: And face the music.
Reader Eleven: There is no place like home.

Chapter Five

Food Fun

There is nothing like cooking or baking to enliven the classroom. Math concepts, such as fractions, can be easily introduced, along with concepts such as the importance following directions and the correct sequence. Pair these scripts with cooking or eating activities. Add cooking-related props or simple costume touches such as chef hats or aprons.

Do You Know the Muffin Man?

Introduce this by talking about muffins, asking students to identify their favorites. If possible, bring in muffins for a snack that day. Ask if they remember a rhyme that talks about getting muffins from a muffin man. Discuss how vendors used to sell their wares on the city streets many years ago, contrasting this to where people get groceries today. (Students familiar with the movie *Shrek* may recall that the Gingerbread Man claimed his father was the Muffin Man, who appeared in the sequel, *Shrek 2*.) *Historical note:* Drury Lane is a London street. The muffin man would sell muffins door to door during Victorian London. The muffins of that day were more consistent with English muffins.

Eating Green Peas

This repetitive script has abundant rhythm and will be easy for students to learn. Have the whole class learn the entire script before assigning readers. *Historical note:* The Civil War song, which inspired the script, describes soldiers eating goober peas, longing to go home. The words and music are attributed to A. Pindar and P. Nutt, respectively, and can be found online using most search engines.

Old Mother Hubbard

Read aloud a traditional version of the rhyme, available in a variety of picture books from the library. Discuss the silliness of the story, how unlikely it is that a dog would ride a goat, wear a wig, or dance a jig. Then tell the students that you are going to read aloud another version, asking them to imagine that all the animals in this version live in Old Mother Hubbard's house. Before reading the last verse, ask the students what they would do if all these animals invaded their house—then read what she did. Students can easily create more verses by choosing additional animals and the food they would eat. *Historical note:* J. Harris published *The Comic Adventures of Old Mother Hubbard and her Dog* in 1805, and the book was immensely popular.

Pease Porridge Hot

The first verse is familiar, offering an easy pattern to learn and expand upon. If preferred, have one student read the first line, triggering the audience to recite the rest of the verse with the students. *Historical note:* Often thought of as similar to oatmeal, it is a traditional baked vegetable dish of mostly yellow peas from England. The rhyme is often used as a clapping game.

Eating Green Peas

Reader One: Sitting by the roadside

Reader Two: On a summer day.

Reader Three: Talking with my friends

Reader Four: Passing time away.

Reader Five: Lying in the shadow

Reader Six: Underneath the trees.

Reader Seven: Yum, yum, yum, yum.

Reader Eight: Eating green peas!

Reader Nine: Peas! Peas! Peas! Peas!

Reader Ten: Eating green peas!

Reader Eleven: Peas! Peas! Peas! Peas!

Reader Twelve: Pass the peas please!

Reader One: Sitting by the roadside

Reader Two: On a summer day.

Reader Three: Talking with my friends

Reader Four: Passing time away.

Reader Five: Lying in the grass

Reader Six: Underneath the sun.

Reader Seven: Yum, yum, yum, yum.

Reader Eight: Eating peas is fun!

Reader Nine: Peas! Peas! Peas! Peas!

Reader Ten: Eating green peas!

Reader Eleven: Peas! Peas! Peas! Peas!

Reader Twelve: Pass the peas please!

Reader One: Sitting by the roadside
Reader Two: On a summer day,
Reader Three: Talking with my friends
Reader Four: Passing time away,
Reader Five: Lying in the grass
Reader Six: All my chores are done.
Reader Seven: Yum, yum, yum, yum.
Reader Eight: Eating peas is fun!
Reader Nine: Peas! Peas! Peas! Peas!
Reader Ten: Eating green peas!
Reader Eleven: Peas! Peas! Peas! Peas!
Reader Twelve: Pass the peas please!

Reader One: Sitting by the poolside
Reader Two: On a summer day,
Reader Three: Talking with my friends
Reader Four: Passing time away,
Reader Five: Lying on a towel
Reader Six: In a summer breeze.
Reader Seven: Yum, yum, yum, yum.
Reader Eight: Eating green peas!
Reader Nine: Peas! Peas! Peas! Peas!
Reader Ten: Eating green peas!
Reader Eleven: Peas! Peas! Peas! Peas!
Reader Twelve: Pass the peas please!

Do You Know the Muffin Man?

Reader One: Do you know the muffin man,
Reader Two: The muffin man, the muffin man?
Reader Three: Do you know the muffin man,
Reader Four: Who lives down Drury Lane?

Reader One: Yes, I know the muffin man,
Reader Two: The muffin man, the muffin man.
Reader Three: Yes, I down the muffin man,
Reader Four: Who lives down Drury Lane.

Reader One: Have you seen the muffin man,
Reader Two: The muffin man, the muffin man?
Reader Three: Have you seen the muffin man,
Reader Four: Who lives down Drury Lane?

Reader One: Yes, I see the muffin man,
Reader Two: The muffin man, the muffin man.
Reader Three: Yes, I see the muffin man,
Reader Four: Who lives down Drury Lane.

Reader One: We all see the muffin man,
Reader Two: The muffin man, the muffin man.
Reader Three: We all see the muffin man,
Reader Four: Who lives down Drury Lane.

Reader One: Say hello to the muffin man,
Reader Two: The muffin man, the muffin man.
Reader Three: Say hello to the muffin man,
Reader Four: Who lives down Drury Lane.

Reader One: Let's buy muffins from the muffin man,
Reader Two: The muffin man, the muffin man.
Reader Three: Let's buy muffins from the muffin man,
Reader Four: Who lives down Drury Lane.

Reader One: We all bought muffins from the muffin man,
Reader Two: The muffin man, the muffin man.
Reader Three: We all bought muffins from the muffin man,
Reader Four: Who lives down Drury Lane.

Reader One: We all ate muffins from the muffin man,
Reader Two: The muffin man, the muffin man.
Reader Three: We all ate muffins from the muffin man,
Reader Four: Who lives down Drury Lane.

Reader One: Say goodbye to the muffin man,
Reader Two: The muffin man, the muffin man.
Reader Three: Say goodbye to the muffin man,
Reader Four: Who lives down Drury Lane.

Old Mother Hubbard

Reader One: Old Mother Hubbard

Reader Two: Went to the cupboard

Reader Three: To get her poor doggie a bone.

Reader Four: When she got there

Reader Five: The cupboard was bare

Reader Six: So the poor little doggie had none.

Reader One: Old Mother Hubbard

Reader Two: Went to the cupboard

Reader Three: To get her poor chicks some corn.

Reader Four: When she got there

Reader Five: The cupboard was bare

Reader Six: So the poor little chicks had none.

Reader One: Old Mother Hubbard

Reader Two: Went to the cupboard

Reader Three: To get her poor kitty some tuna.

Reader Four: When she got there

Reader Five: The cupboard was bare

Reader Six: So the poor little kitty had none.

Reader One: Old Mother Hubbard

Reader Two: Went to the cupboard

Reader Three: To get her poor pony some grain.

Reader Four: When she got there

Reader Five: The cupboard was bare

Reader Six: So the poor little pony had none.

Reader One: Old Mother Hubbard

Reader Two: Went to the cupboard

Reader Three: To get her poor cow some hay.

Reader Four: When she got there

Reader Five: The cupboard was bare

Reader Six: So the poor little cow had none.

Reader One: Old Mother Hubbard

Reader Two: Went to the cupboard

Reader Three: To get her poor mouse some cheese.

Reader Four: When she got there

Reader Five: The cupboard was bare

Reader Six: So the poor little mouse had none.

Reader One: Old Mother Hubbard

Reader Two: Went to the cupboard

Reader Three: To get her poor fish some worms.

Reader Four: When she got there

Reader Five: The cupboard was bare

Reader Six: So the poor little fish had none.

Reader One: Old Mother Hubbard

Reader Two: Went to the cupboard

Reader Three: To get her poor parrot some seeds.

Reader Four: When she got there

Reader Five: The cupboard was bare

Reader Six: So the poor little parrot had none.

Reader One: Old Mother Hubbard

Reader Two: Went to the cupboard

Reader Three: To get her poor goat some cans.

Reader Four: When she got there

Reader Five: The cupboard was bare

Reader Six: So the poor little goat had none.

Reader One: Old Mother Hubbard

Reader Two: Went to the cupboard

Reader Three: To get her poor monkey some bananas.

Reader Four: When she got there

Reader Five: The cupboard was bare

Reader Six: So the poor little monkey had none.

Reader One: Old Mother Hubbard

Reader Two: Went to the cupboard

Reader Three: To get her poor elephant some leaves.

Reader Four: When she got there

Reader Five: The cupboard was bare

Reader Six: So the poor little elephant had none.

Reader One: Old Mother Hubbard

Reader Two: Went to the cupboard

Reader Three: To get her poor tiger some meat.

Reader Four: When she got there

Reader Five: The cupboard was bare

Reader Six: So the poor little tiger had none.

Reader One: Old Mother Hubbard

Reader Two: Went to the cupboard

Reader Three: To get her poor self some food.

Reader Four: When she got there

Reader Five: The cupboard was bare

Reader Six: So Mother Hubbard left home alone!

Pease Porridge Hot

Reader One: Pease porridge hot.
Reader Two: Pease porridge cold.
Reader Three: Pease porridge in the pot.
Reader Four: Nine days old.
Reader Five: Some like it hot.
Reader Six: Some like it cold.
Reader Seven: Some like it in the pot.
Reader Eight: Nine days old.

Reader One: Chicken dumplings hot.
Reader Two: Chicken dumplings cold.
Reader Three: Chicken dumplings in the pot.
Reader Four: Nine days old.
Reader Five: Some like it hot.
Reader Six: Some like it cold.
Reader Seven: Some like it in the pot.
Reader Eight: Nine days old.

Reader One: Beef stew hot.
Reader Two: Beef stew cold.
Reader Three: Beef stew in the pot.
Reader Four: Nine days old.
Reader Five: Some like it hot.
Reader Six: Some like it cold.
Reader Seven: Some like it in the pot.
Reader Eight: Nine days old.

Reader One: Curry rice hot.

Reader Two: Curry rice cold.

Reader Three: Curry rice in the pot.

Reader Four: Nine days old.

Reader Five: Some like it hot.

Reader Six: Some like it cold.

Reader Seven: Some like it in the pot.

Reader Eight: Nine days old.

Reader One: Vegetable soup hot.

Reader Two: Vegetable soup cold.

Reader Three: Vegetable soup in the pot.

Reader Four: Nine days old.

Reader Five: Some like it hot.

Reader Six: Some like it cold.

Reader Seven: Some like it in the pot.

Reader Eight: Nine days old.

Reader One: Baked beans hot.

Reader Two: Baked beans cold.

Reader Three: Baked beans in the pot.

Reader Four: Nine days old.

Reader Five: Some like it hot.

Reader Six: Some like it cold.

Reader Seven: Some like it in the pot.

Reader Eight: Nine days old.

Reader One: Spaghetti sauce hot.
Reader Two: Spaghetti sauce cold.
Reader Three: Spaghetti sauce in the pot.
Reader Four: Nine days old.
Reader Five: Some like it hot.

Reader Six: Some like it cold.
Reader Seven: Some like it in the pot.
Reader Eight: Nine days old.

Reader One: Roast pork hot.
Reader Two: Roast pork cold.
Reader Three: Roast pork in the pot.
Reader Four: Nine days old.
Reader Five: Some like it hot.
Reader Six: Some like it cold.
Reader Seven: Some like it in the pot.
Reader Eight: Nine days old.

Chapter Six

Music and Movement

These scripts provide opportunities to sing and move, especially useful for when students need to work out the wiggles. Teach them as rhymes first, introducing each on chart paper or on the chalkboard. Add motions as appropriate. When the students have mastered reciting them, give students the scripts and use them as readers theatre. Consider adding rhythm instruments to the reading.

As I Was Going Up the Hill

Once the students or audience learns the pattern, the second verse to each set could be recited in a call-and-response pattern. *Historical note:* The original version specifies petticoats instead of socks in the fourth line, c. 1850.

The Bear Went over the Mountain

Sung to the tune of "For He's a Jolly Good Fellow," this popular children's song is expanded with the bear visiting many other places. Teach the children the song before introducing the script.

Ding Dong Bell

If preferred, while Readers One through Five are reading their lines, have Readers Six through Ten pantomime the action or use rhythm instruments while the lines are read. Encourage the students to create additional verses.

Down by the Station

Children familiar with this train song will enjoy the expansion to a variety of other vehicles and locations. Teach the students the song before teaching the script.

I Stand inside a Circle

Have the class make a circle with the readers inside their classmates. While the readers read the lines, the other students dance, walk, clap, and the like. After the first verse, cue the students to the upcoming verse by stating "Dance" after verse one, "Walk" after verse two, and so forth. Use this script when students need a break.

If All the Seas Were One Sea

Explore a variety of locations by starting with the traditional verses. *Historical note:* Reputedly, Rowland Hill (1744–1833), a renowned preacher, used the story of a great man with a great axe as part of a sermon.

It's All Fun

This script offers another opportunity to pantomime the actions while the students read the lines.

I've Been Working on the Railroad

Create additional verses by adding types of workers. Substitute names of students throughout the song, if preferred. *Historical note:* This American folk song originally may have been about working on a levee instead of a railroad.

The Swing

Discuss what students can see when they are swinging high. Inspired by Robert Louis Stevenson's poem, "The Swing," encourage students to create additional verses.

As I Was Going Up the Hill

Reader One: As I was going up the hill
Reader Two: I met with Jack the piper.
Reader Three: The only tune that he could play
Reader Four: Was "Tie your socks up tighter."

Reader Five: I tied them once. I tied them twice.
Reader Six: I tied them three times over.
Reader Seven: And the only song that he could sing
Reader Eight: Was "Carry me safe to Dover."

Reader One: As I was going up the hill
Reader Two: I met with Sue the singer.
Reader Three: The only song that she could sing
Reader Four: Was "Tie up your bells with your finger."

Reader Five: I tied them once. I tied them twice.
Reader Six: I tied them three times over.
Reader Seven: And the only song that she could sing
Reader Eight: Was "Carry me safe to Dover."

Reader One: As I was going up the hill
Reader Two: I met with Sam the sailor.
Reader Three: The only song that he could sing
Reader Four: Was "Tie up your sails. There's a gale, Sir."

Reader Five: I tied them once. I tied them twice.
Reader Six: I tied them three times over.
Reader Seven: And the only song that he could sing
Reader Eight: Was "Carry me safe to Dover."

Reader One: As I was going up the hill
Reader Two: I met with Barb the baker.
Reader Three: The only song that she could sing
Reader Four: Was "Mix up your bread with a shaker."

Reader Five: I mixed it once. I mixed it twice.
Reader Six: I mixed it three times over.
Reader Seven: And the only song that she could sing
Reader Eight: Was "Carry me safe to Dover."

Reader One: As I was going up the hill
Reader Two: I met with Herb the hiker.
Reader Three: The only song that he could sing
Reader Four: Was "I wish you were a biker."

Reader Five: I biked it once. I biked it twice.
Reader Six: I biked it three times over.
Reader Seven: And the only song that he could sing
Reader Eight: Was "Carry me safe to Dover."

Reader One: As I was going up the hill
Reader Two: I met with Rob the racer.
Reader Three: The only song that he could sing
Reader Four: Was "Do you think that you can chase her?"

Reader Five: I chased him once. I chased him twice.
Reader Six: I chased him three times over.
Reader Seven: And the only song that he could sing
Reader Eight: Was "Carry me safe to Dover."

Reader One: As I was going up the hill
Reader Two: I met with a banjo strummer.
Reader Three: The only tune that she could play
Reader Four: Was "I wish that I were a drummer."

Reader Five: I strummed with her once. I strummed with her twice.

Reader Six: I strummed with her three times over.

Reader Seven: And the only song that she could play

Reader Eight: Was "Carry me safe to Dover."

Reader One: As I was going down the hill

Reader Two: I met a man going home.

Reader Three: The only song that he could sing

Reader Four: Was "I just don't want to roam."

Reader Five: I sang with him once. I sang with him twice.

Reader Six: I sang with him three times over.

Reader Seven: And the only song that he could sing

Reader Eight: Was "Carry me safe to Dover."

The Bear Went over the Mountain

Reader One: The bear went over the mountain.

Reader Two: The bear went over the mountain.

Reader Three: The bear went over the mountain.

Reader Four: To see what he could see.

Reader Five: And all that he could see.

Reader Six: And all that he could see.

Reader Seven: Was the other side of the mountain.

Reader Eight: The other side of the mountain.

Reader Nine: The other side of the mountain.

Reader Ten: Was all that he could see.

Reader One: The bear went into the forest.

Reader Two: The bear went into the forest.

Reader Three: The bear went into the forest.

Reader Four: To see what he could see.

Reader Five: And all that he could see.

Reader Six: And all that he could see.

Reader Seven: Was the other side of the forest.

Reader Eight: The other side of the forest

Reader Nine: The other side of the forest.

Reader Ten: Was all that he could see.

Reader One: The bear went into the jungle.

Reader Two: The bear went into the jungle.

Reader Three: The bear went into the jungle.

Reader Four: To see what he could see.

Reader Five: And all that he could see.

Reader Six: And all that he could see.

Reader Seven: Was the other side of the jungle.

Reader Eight: The other side of the jungle.
Reader Nine: The other side of the jungle.
Reader Ten: Was all that he could see.

Reader One: The bear went over the ocean.
Reader Two: The bear went over the ocean.
Reader Three: The bear went over the ocean.
Reader Four: To see what he could see.
Reader Five: And all that he could see.
Reader Six: And all that he could see.
Reader Seven: Was the other side of the ocean.
Reader Eight: The other side of the ocean.
Reader Nine: The other side of the ocean.
Reader Ten: Was all that he could see.

Reader One: The bear went through the city.
Reader Two: The bear went through the city.
Reader Three: The bear went through the city.
Reader Four: To see what he could see.
Reader Five: And all that he could see.
Reader Six: And all that he could see.
Reader Seven: Was the other side of the city.
Reader Eight: The other side of the city.
Reader Nine: The other side of the city.
Reader Ten: Was all that he could see.

Reader One: The bear went into the river.
Reader Two: The bear went into the river.
Reader Three: The bear went into the river.
Reader Four: To see what he could see.
Reader Five: And all that he could see.
Reader Six: And all that he could see.
Reader Seven: Were the fishes in the river.

Reader Eight: The fishes in the river.
Reader Nine: The fishes in the river.
Reader Ten: Were all that he could see.

Reader One: The bear went past the farm.
Reader Two: The bear went past the farm.
Reader Three: The bear went past the farm.
Reader Four: To see what he could see.
Reader Five: And all that he could see.
Reader Six: And all that he could see.
Reader Seven: Was the other side of the farm.
Reader Eight: The other side of the farm.
Reader Nine: The other side of the farm.
Reader Ten: Was all that he could see.

Reader One: The bear back to the mountain.
Reader Two: The bear back to the mountain.
Reader Three: The bear back to the mountain.
Reader Four: To see what he could see.
Reader Five: And all that he could see.
Reader Six: And all that he could see.
Reader Seven: Was his favorite side of the mountain.
Reader Eight: His favorite side of the mountain.
Reader Nine: His favorite side of the mountain.
Reader Ten: Was all that he could see.

Ding Dong Bell

Reader One: Ding dong, ding dong, ding dong bell.

Reader Two: Ding dong bell.

Reader Three: Ding dong, ding dong bell.

Reader Four: Hear the merry, merry bells.

Reader Five: They ring a ding dong song.

Reader Six: Tip tap, tip tap, tip tap sticks.

Reader Seven: Tip tap sticks.

Reader Eight: Tip tap, tip tap sticks.

Reader Nine: Hear the playful, playful sticks.

Reader Ten: They hit a tip tap drum.

Reader One: Click clack, click clack, click clack train.

Reader Two: Click clack train.

Reader Three: Click clack, click clack train.

Reader Four: Hear the noisy, noisy train.

Reader Five: It rides across the plain.

Reader Six: Drip drop, drip drop, drip drop rain.

Reader Seven: Drip drop rain.

Reader Eight: Drip drop, drip drop rain.

Reader Nine: Hear the happy, happy rain.

Reader Ten: It falls down in the lane.

Reader One: Step hop, step hop, step hop feet

Reader Two: Step hop feet.

Reader Three: Step hop, step hop feet.

Reader Four: Hear the lively, lively feet.

Reader Five: They cross the busy street.

Reader Six: Down up, down up, down up swing.

Reader Seven: Down up swing.

Reader Eight: Down up, down up swing.

Reader Nine: Feel the blowing, blowing air.

Reader Ten: In my down up chair.

Reader One: Spin sway, spin sway, spin sway dance.

Reader Two: Spin sway dance.

Reader Three: Spin sway, spin sway dance.

Reader Four: See the turning, turning girls.

Reader Five: They spin a spinning dance.

Reader Six: Clap clap, clap clap, clap clap hands.

Reader Seven: Clap clap hands

Reader Eight: Clap clap, clap clap hands.

Reader Nine: See our play is done, done, done.

Reader Ten: So clap clap, clap clap hands.

Down by the Station

Reader One: Down by the station
Reader Two: Early in the morning.
Reader Three: See the little puffer bellies
Reader Four: All in a row.
Reader Five: See the station master
Reader Six: Turn a little handle.
Reader Seven: Chug, chug, puff, puff.
Reader Eight: Off they go.

Reader One: Down by the river
Reader Two: Early in the morning.
Reader Three: See the great big barges
Reader Four: All in a row.
Reader Five: See the barge captains
Reader Six: Turn a little handle.
Reader Seven: Swish, swish, through the waves.
Reader Eight: Off they go.

Reader One: Down by the schoolyard
Reader Two: Early in the morning.
Reader Three: See the yellow buses
Reader Four: All in a row.
Reader Five: See the bus drivers
Reader Six: Turn a little handle.
Reader Seven: Honk, honk, close the doors.
Reader Eight: Off they go.

Reader One: Down by the seashore
Reader Two: Early in the morning.
Reader Three: See the pretty sailboats
Reader Four: All in a row.
Reader Five: See the sailboat captains
Reader Six: Turn a little handle.
Reader Seven: Flap, flap, in the wind.
Reader Eight: Off they go.

Reader One: Down by the playground
Reader Two: Early in the morning.
Reader Three: See the baby strollers
Reader Four: All in a row.
Reader Five: See the happy mommies
Reader Six: Turn a little handle.
Reader Seven: Swing high, swing low.
Reader Eight: Off they go.

Reader One: Down by the city
Reader Two: Early in the morning.
Reader Three: See the yellow taxis
Reader Four: All in a row.
Reader Five: See the taxi drivers
Reader Six: Turn a little handle.
Reader Seven: Toot, toot, down the streets.
Reader Eight: Off they go.

Reader One: Down by the farmyard

Reader Two: Early in the morning.

Reader Three: See the little tractors

Reader Four: All in a row.

Reader Five: See the happy farmers

Reader Six: Turn a little handle.

Reader Seven: Mow, mow down the rows.

Reader Eight: Off they go.

Reader One: Back at the house.

Reader Two: Early in the evening.

Reader Three: See the tired children.

Reader Four: All in a row.

Reader Five: See the sleepy daddy

Reader Six: Read a little story.

Reader Seven: Shh, shh, time to dream.

Reader Eight: Off they go.

I Stand inside a Circle

Reader One: I stand inside a circle.
Reader Two: All around me are my friends.
Reader Three: You stand inside a circle.
Reader Four: And all around you are your friends.

Reader One: I dance inside a circle.
Reader Two: All around me are my friends.
Reader Three: You dance inside a circle.
Reader Four: And all around you are your friends.

Reader One: I walk inside a circle.
Reader Two: All around me are my friends.
Reader Three: You walk inside a circle.
Reader Four: And all around you are your friends.

Reader One: I clap hands in a circle.
Reader Two: All around me are my friends.
Reader Three: You clap hands in a circle.
Reader Four: And all around you are your friends.

Reader One: I sing inside a circle.
Reader Two: All around me are my friends.
Reader Three: You sing inside a circle.
Reader Four: And all around you are your friends.

Reader One: I skip inside a circle.
Reader Two: All around me are my friends.
Reader Three: You skip inside a circle.
Reader Four: And all around you are your friends.

Reader One: I hear a story in a circle.
Reader Two: All around me are my friends.
Reader Three: You hear a story in a circle.
Reader Four: And all around you are your friends.

Reader One: I hop inside a circle.
Reader Two: All around me are my friends.
Reader Three: You hop inside a circle.
Reader Four: And all around you are your friends.

Reader One: I nap inside a circle.
Reader Two: All around me are my friends.
Reader Three: You nap inside a circle.
Reader Four: And all around you are your friends.

Reader One: I dream inside a circle.
Reader Two: All around me are my friends.
Reader Three: You dream inside a circle.
Reader Four: And all around you are your friends.

Reader One: I wake up inside a circle.
Reader Two: All around me are my friends.
Reader Three: You wake up inside a circle.
Reader Four: And all around you are your friends.

Reader One: I gallop inside a circle.
Reader Two: All around me are my friends.
Reader Three: You gallop inside a circle.
Reader Four: And all around you are your friends.

Reader One: I hop inside a circle.
Reader Two: All around me are my friends.
Reader Three: You hop inside a circle.
Reader Four: And all around you are your friends.

Reader One: I whisper inside a circle.

Reader Two: All around me are my friends.

Reader Three: You whisper inside a circle.

Reader Four: And all around you are your friends.

Reader One: I hug inside a circle.

Reader Two: All around me are my friends.

Reader Three: You hug inside a circle.

Reader Four: And all around you are your friends.

Reader One: I march inside a circle.

Reader Two: All around me are my friends.

Reader Three: You march inside a circle.

Reader Four: And all around you are your friends.

Reader One: I wave inside a circle.

Reader Two: And say goodbye to my friends.

Reader Three: You wave inside a circle.

Reader Four: And say goodbye to your friends.

Everyone (waving): Goodbye!

If All the Seas Were One Sea

Reader One: If all the seas were one sea,
Reader Two: What a great sea that would be.
Reader Three: If all the trees were one tree,
Reader Four: What a great tree that would be.

Reader Five: If all the axes were one ax,
Reader Six: What a great ax that would be.
Reader Seven: If all the men were one man,
Reader Eight: What a great man that would be.

Reader Nine: And if that great man took the great ax,
Reader Ten: And cut down the great tree.
Reader Eleven: And let it fall in the great sea.
Reader Twelve: What a great splash that would be.

Reader One: If all the mountains were one mountain,
Reader Two: What a great mountain that would be.
Reader Three: If all the forests were one forest,
Reader Four: What a great forest that would be.

Reader Five: If all the axes were one ax,
Reader Six: What a great ax that would be.
Reader Seven: If all the loggers were one logger,
Reader Eight: What a great logger that would be.

Reader Nine: And if that great logger took the great ax,
Reader Ten: And cut down those great trees.
Reader Eleven: And let them fall in the great forest,
Reader Twelve: What a great crash that would be.

Reader One: If all the deserts were one desert,
Reader Two: What a great desert that would be.
Reader Three: If all the cacti were one cacti,
Reader Four: What a great cacti that would be.

Reader Five: If all the axes were one ax,
Reader Six: What a great ax that would be.
Reader Seven: If all the women were one woman,
Reader Eight: What a great woman that would be.

Reader Nine: And if that great woman took the great ax,
Reader Ten: And chopped it, one, two, three.
Reader Eleven: And the cactus fell in the great desert,
Reader Twelve: What a great feat that would be.

Reader One: If all the jungles were one jungle,
Reader Two: What a great jungle that would be.
Reader Three: If all the vines were one vine,
Reader Four: What a great vine that would be.

Reader Five: If all the axes were one ax,
Reader Six: What a great ax that would be.
Reader Seven: If all the monkeys were one monkey,
Reader Eight: What a great monkey that would be.

Reader Nine: And if that great monkey took that great ax,
Reader Ten: And chopped the vine with glee.
Reader Eleven: And let it fall in the great jungle,
Reader Twelve: What a great mess that would be.

Reader One: If all the seas were one sea,
Reader Two: What a great sea that would be.
Reader Three: If all the trees were one tree,
Reader Four: What a great tree that would be.

Reader Five: If all the axes were one ax,
Reader Six: What a great ax that would be.
Reader Seven: If all the men were one man,
Reader Eight: What a great man that would be.

Reader Nine: And if that great man took the great ax,
Reader Ten: And cut down the great tree.
Reader Eleven: And let it fall in the great sea.
Reader Twelve: What a great splash that would be.

 # It's All Fun!

Reader One: Reading is fun.
Reader Two: A, B, C, D.
Reader Three: Learning and earning
Reader Four: Will never be done.

Reader Five: Jumping is fun.
Reader Six: Up, down, up, down.
Reader Seven: Hopping and popping
Reader Eight: Will never be done.

Reader One: Hiking is fun.
Reader Two: One, two, three, four.
Reader Three: Camping and tramping
Reader Four: Will never be done.

Reader Five: Biking is fun.
Reader Six: Pump, pump, pump, pump.
Reader Seven: Going and slowing
Reader Eight: Will never be done.

Reader One: Dancing is fun.
Reader Two: In and out, in and out.
Reader Three: Swaying and playing
Reader Four: Will never be done.

Reader Five: Eating is fun.
Reader Six: Yum, yum, yum, yum.
Reader Seven: Tasting and basting
Reader Eight: Will never be done.

Reader One: Swinging is fun.
Reader Two: High, low, high, low
Reader Three: Riding and gliding
Reader Four: Will never be done.

Reader Five: Skating is fun.
Reader Six: On the ice, in the snow.
Reader Seven: Falling and calling
Reader Eight: Will never be done.

Reader One: Singing is fun.
Reader Two: La, la, la, la.
Reader Three: Humming and thrumming
Reader Four: Will never be done.

Reader Five: Marching is fun.
Reader Six: Left, right, left, right.
Reader Seven: Drumming and strumming
Reader Eight: Will never be done.

Reader One: Prancing is fun.
Reader Two: Kick high. Kick low.
Reader Three: Skipping and tripping
Reader Four: Will never be done.

Reader Five: Sleeping is fun.
Reader Six: Zzz, zzz, zzz, zzz.
Reader Seven: Resting and nesting
Reader Eight: And now we are done.

I've Been Working on the Railroad

Reader One: I've been working on the railroad,

Reader Two: All the livelong day.

Reader Three: I've been working on the railroad,

Reader Four: Just to pass the time away.

Reader Five: Don't you hear the whistle blowing?

Reader Six: Rise up so early in the morn.

Reader Seven: Don't you hear the captain shouting?

Reader Eight: Dinah, blow your horn.

Reader One: Dinah, won't you blow?

Reader Two: Dinah, won't you blow?

Reader Three: Dinah, won't you blow your horn?

Reader Four: Dinah, won't you blow?

Readers Five and Six: Dinah, won't you blow?

Readers Seven and Eight: Dinah, won't you blow your horn?

Reader One: I've been working in the shipyard,

Reader Two: All the livelong day.

Reader Three: I've been working in the shipyard,

Reader Four: Just to pass the time away.

Reader Five: Don't you hear the whistle blowing?

Reader Six: Rise up so early in the morn.

Reader Seven: Don't you hear the captain shouting?

Reader Eight: Jessie, blow your horn.

Reader One: Jessie, won't you blow?

Reader Two: Jessie, won't you blow?

Reader Three: Jessie, won't you blow your horn?

Reader Four: Jessie, won't you blow?

Readers Five and Six: Jessie, won't you blow?

Readers Seven and Eight: Jessie, won't you blow your horn?

Reader One: I've been working in the farmyard,

Reader Two: All the livelong day.

Reader Three: I've been working in the farmyard,

Reader Four: Just to pass the time away.

Reader Five: Don't you hear the rooster crowing?

Reader Six: Rise up so early in the morn.

Reader Seven: Don't you hear the rooster crowing?

Reader Eight: Molly, blow your horn.

Reader One: Molly, won't you blow?

Reader Two: Molly, won't you blow?

Reader Three: Molly, won't you blow your horn?

Reader Four: Molly, won't you blow?

Readers Five and Six: Molly, won't you blow?

Readers Seven and Eight: Molly, won't you blow your horn?

Reader One: I've been working in the factory,

Reader Two: All the livelong day.

Reader Three: I've been working in the factory,

Reader Four: Just to pass the time away.

Reader Five: Don't you hear the foreman shouting?

Reader Six: Rise up so early in the morn.

Reader Seven: Don't you hear the foreman shouting?

Reader Eight: Joshua, blow your horn.

Reader One: Joshua, won't you blow?

Reader Two: Joshua, won't you blow?

Reader Three: Joshua, won't you blow your horn?

Reader Four: Joshua, won't you blow?

Readers Five and Six: Joshua, won't you blow?

Readers Seven and Eight: Joshua, won't you blow your horn?

Reader One: I stopped working on the railroad,

Reader Two: All the livelong day.

Reader Three: I stopped working on the railroad,

Reader Four: Just to pass the time away.

Reader Five: I don't hear the whistle blowing.

Reader Six: I won't rise so early in the morn.

Reader Seven: No more hearing the captain shouting.

Reader Eight: Dinah, blow your horn.

Reader One: Dinah, please don't blow.

Reader Two: Dinah, please don't blow.

Reader Three: Dinah, please don't blow your horn.

Reader Four: Dinah, please don't blow.

Readers Five and Six: Dinah, please don't blow.

Readers Seven and Eight: Dinah please don't blow your horn.

 # The Swing

Reader One: How do you like to go up in a swing?
Reader Two: Up in the air so blue.
Reader Three: Oh, I do think it is the nicest thing
Reader Four: Ever a child can do!

Reader One: I look down on the garden green.
Reader Two: Down on the plants so green.
Reader Three: Up in the air I go flying again.
Reader Four: The prettiest garden I've seen!

Reader One: I look down on the roof of my house.
Reader Two: Down on the roof so brown.
Reader Three: Up in the air I go flying again.
Reader Four: Up in the air and down!

Reader One: I look down on the yard next door.
Reader Two: Down on the yard so fine.
Reader Three: Up in the air I go flying again.
Reader Four: I wish the yard were mine!

Reader One: I look down on the river
Reader Two: That runs next to our town.
Reader Three: Up in the air I go flying again.
Reader Four: Up in the air and down!

Reader One: I look down on the trees
Reader Two: With leaves turning gold.
Reader Three: Up in the air I go flying again.
Reader Four: Swinging can never get old.

Reader One: I look down on the cattle

Reader Two: Who are walking down the lane.

Reader Three: Up in the air I go flying again.

Reader Four: The cows go home to eat grain!

Reader One: I look down on my friends

Reader Two: Who are playing in the park.

Reader Three: Up in the air I go flying again.

Reader Four: I can swing till it's dark!

Reader One: I go up and over the wall,

Reader Two: Till I can see the whole town,

Reader Three: Up in the air I go flying again.

Reader Four: Up in the air and down!

Index

About the Authors

SUZANNE I. BARCHERS Ed.D., has written fifty books, ranging from college textbooks to children's books. (See books and other readers theatre scripts at www.storycart.com.) Currently the Editor in Chief and Vice President of Leapfrog, she has served as a public school teacher, an affiliate faculty for the University of Colorado, Denver, an acquisitions editor for Teacher Ideas Press, and Managing Editor at Weekly Reader. She also serves on the PBS Kids Media Advisory Board and is a past member of the board of directors for the Association of Educational Publishers (EdPress).

CHARLA R. PFEFFINGER received her bachelor of science degree in elementary education and her master's degree in reading from Illinois State University, Normal, Illinois. Mrs. Pfeffinger was an educator in Illinois for twenty-two years before retiring. She has been a contributing author to *Learning* magazine, Storycart Press, and the author of *A Teen's Book of Lists, Holiday Readers Theatre*, and *Character Counts! Promoting Character Education: Readers Theatre*.